ORGANIC CANNABIS CULTIVATION

A Complete Beginner-To-Intermediate Guide For Growing Cannabis Organically

BY MR. GROW IT

Organic Cannabis Cultivation: A Complete Beginner-To-Intermediate Guide For Growing Cannabis Organically, 1st Edition
Copyright © 2024 by Mr. Grow It

ISBN: 978-1-7351961-2-1

Cover photo: @video.macro, Jealousy grown by @notillkings

Principle photography © Mr. Grow It

Additional photography by: KIS Organics, Matt Powers, HomeGrowTV, Tony Fernandez, Matthew Gates (Zenthanol Consulting), Robert Rankin, @McCannabisLuke, @typ3cannabis

All rights reserved. No part of this book may be reproduced, distributed, or transmitted in any form or by any means, including photocopying, recording, or other electronic or mechanical methods, without the prior written permission of the author, except in the case of brief quotations embodied in critical reviews and certain other noncommercial uses permitted by copyright law. For permission requests, email the author, addressed "Attention: Permission Request", at the address below.

contact@mrgrowit.com

Visit www.MrGrowIt.com

DISCLAIMER:
This book is meant to provide information about growing cannabis. The content in this book is for educational purposes only. The legal aspects of growing cannabis vary in different countries. Hence, readers are advised to use their own discretion and abide by the laws of their country for growing cannabis. The author does not advocate breaking the law. The use of any information provided in this book is solely at your own risk. Although every precaution has been taken to verify the accuracy of the information contained herein, the author assumes no responsibility for any errors or omissions. No liability is assumed for damages that may result from the use of information contained within.

To my future wife, Samantha, and our beautiful daughter, Emma, may our journey together be as fun and rewarding as the organic gardens we cultivate.

TABLE OF Contents

INTRODUCTION	6
Chapter 1: ORGANIC VS SYNTHETIC	9
Chapter 2: ESSENTIAL ELEMENTS	14
Chapter 3: EQUIPMENT CHECKLIST	18
Chapter 4: SOIL	24
Chapter 5: CONTAINERS	31
Chapter 6: BASE INPUTS	38
Chapter 7: LIGHTING	44
Chapter 8: ENVIRONMENT	49
Chapter 9: WATER	55
Chapter 10: MICROBES	62
Chapter 11: PEST PREVENTION	71
Chapter 12: COMPOST TEAS	78
Chapter 13: COVER CROPS	86
Chapter 14: MULCH LAYERS	91
Chapter 15: COMPANION PLANTING	96
Chapter 16: EARTHWORMS	102
Chapter 17: BENEFICIAL INSECTS	108
Chapter 18: COMPOSTING	113
Chapter 19: SOIL RECIPES	122
Chapter 20: FERTILIZERS & AMENDMENTS	128

Alfalfa Meal	130
Azomite	131
Bat Guano	133
Blood Meal	134
Bone Meal	135
Cottonseed Meal	136
Crustacean Meal	138
Feather Meal	139
Fish Hydrolysate	141
Fish Meal	142
Greensand	144
Humic Acid	145
Insect Frass	147
Kelp Meal	148
Langbeinite	150
Neem Seed Meal	151
Oyster Shells	153
Rock Phosphate	154
Seabird Guano	155
Soybean Meal	157
Chapter 21: DIY FERTILIZERS	**160**
Eggshells Calcium Fertilizer	162
Banana Peels Potassium Fertilizer	164
Fermented Plant Juice & Fermented Fruit Juice	166
Chapter 22: COMMON PROBLEMS & SOLUTIONS	**170**
EPILOGUE	178
GLOSSARY	180

INTRODUCTION

Welcome to the world of eco-friendly gardening! By purchasing this book, you've taken a significant step toward sustainable gardening.

Whether you are a complete beginner, transitioning from synthetic nutrients to organic practices, or an aspiring organic grower looking to deepen your knowledge, this book caters to various experience levels. It provides the basics of organic gardening for beginners and also includes intermediate knowledge for those who want to dive deeper into the subject. For absolute beginners, I recommend referring to my other book, "7 Steps To Grow Cannabis," which covers fundamental growing methods not addressed in this book. Topics such as equipment setup, seeds, different growth stages, harvest, drying, and curing, are extensively covered in my other book.

Over the past decade, the cannabis cultivation community has expanded significantly, bringing together like-minded individuals who are dedicated to improvement and openly sharing their best practices, making this community a lot of fun to be a part of.

Since the release of my previous book, my knowledge has continued to grow. I earned a Cannabis Cultivation Certificate from Utah State University. I also had the privilege of interviewing over 100 gardeners, including experts in organic gardening, on my Garden Talk podcast. My personal experience with organic gardening has also evolved, with my soil improving over time and keeping plants healthy has become much easier.

While this beginner-to-intermediate guide covers a wide range of organic gardening topics, there is always more to discover. Scientific studies on cannabis cultivation are being conducted more frequently, unveiling new information about the plant each day. Therefore, I encourage you to embrace the principle of "continuous improvement" and avoid thinking you've mastered it all.

It's important to note that this book is not solely based on my personal knowledge and experiences. The information presented here comes from a diverse range of reliable sources. Additionally, I've sought the expertise of several individuals with advanced knowledge in organic cannabis cultivation. My goal is to offer accurate information from credible sources while creating a user-friendly guide that remains relevant for many years to come.

Congratulations on acquiring this book. My hope is that it becomes your essential resource for organic cannabis gardening, helping you grow a healthy and sustainable garden. Best of luck!

CHAPTER 1: ORGANIC VS SYNTHETIC

ORGANIC VS *Synthetic*

*I*n the world of gardening, there are two distinct approaches: organic gardening and synthetic gardening. While both methods share the common goal of growing healthy plants, they differ significantly in their techniques, philosophies, and the products they utilize. While the focus of this book revolves around organic gardening, it is crucial to gain a clear understanding of the true meaning of organic and how it is different from synthetic practices. This chapter aims to reveal the differences between organic and synthetic gardening, focusing on their contrasting growing styles, nutrient sources, and environmental impacts.

ORGANIC

Organic gardening is often regarded as a traditional and natural method of cultivation. It revolves around the use of organic products and avoids synthetic fertilizers and pesticides. The term "organic" refers to carbon-based materials, including various organic fertilizers derived from natural sources such as bone meal or seabird guano – just to name a few. These slow-release fertilizers not only produce nutrition that plants require, but also enhance soil structure and promote the growth of beneficial microorganisms. Organic gardening aims to protect the environment and maintain ecological balance.

SYNTHETIC

Gardening with synthetic inputs involves a more precise and calculated approach. It relies on synthetic or inorganic products such as liquid fertilizers and chemical pesticides. Synthetic fertilizers are typically quick-release and provide nutrients to plants in a readily available form. However, they may sometimes lack essential nutrients for plants, disrupt nutrient balance in the soil, and can harm the development of beneficial soil microorganisms when used excessively. Synthetic gardening requires strict application and monitoring to ensure optimal results.

NUTRIENT ABSORPTION

One of the primary distinctions between organic and synthetic gardening lies in how plants acquire nutrients. Organic gardening relies on organic inputs such as compost, organic amendments, or organic fertilizer blends. These inputs are slowly broken down by microorganisms, converting them into nutrients that the plants can absorb. Derived from natural sources, these inputs promote a healthier soil ecosystem, improve soil structure over time, and help retain moisture.

On the other hand, synthetic gardening uses inputs that are artificially created. For instance, the Haber-Bosch process involves fixing nitrogen with hydrogen to produce ammonia. While efficient in producing ammonia for synthetic fertilizers, this process poses environmental concerns due to its high energy consumption and carbon emissions. Most synthetic inputs are readily available for plant uptake, bypassing the need for microbial breakdown. This leads to a "faster-acting" solution. While synthetic fertilizers can provide immediate benefits, they often fail to enrich the soil and may result in nutrient imbalances and environmental pollution.

GROWING MEDIUM

The choice of growing medium can also vary with organic and synthetic gardening. Organic gardeners typically use soil or a potting mix that incorporates ingredients like peat moss or coco coir for moisture retention, aeration additives such as perlite or rice hulls, and organic matter like compost or worm castings that provide necessary nutrition for plant growth. There are numerous other options that can be included in the mix, many of them we will touch upon throughout this book.

Another option is bagged soil, which can be purchased from local nurseries or hydroponics stores. These mixes are often pre-amended with an organic fertilizer to provide sufficient nutrition for the beginning stages of the plant's life. Organic gardeners will then continue to, "feed the soil" with organic inputs as the plant continues to grow.

Note: Not all organic fertilizers are guaranteed to be safe, as some may contain traces of heavy metals, which can be a significant concern. It is always advisable to choose organic fertilizers that have undergone testing, ensuring that reports are available for you to review, confirming their absence of harmful levels of heavy metals.

On the other hand, synthetic gardeners often prefer an inert medium. An inert grow medium is a type of grow media that contains no nutrients. Some examples are coco coir, rock wool, hydro clay pebbles, perlite, or vermiculite. These mediums do not require pre-amendment and are helpful for precise nutrient delivery systems, including bottled-nutrient lineups that are predominantly derived from synthetic sources.

PROS AND CONS

Both organic and synthetic gardening methods have their advantages and disadvantages. Organic gardening is often praised for its eco-friendly approach, reliance on natural products, and long-term soil improvement. However, it requires more time and effort in soil preparation and may have slower nutrient availability. Synthetic gardening, on the other hand, offers precision and efficiency in nutrient delivery. Although, it can contribute to nutrient imbalances, harm beneficial soil organisms, and have negative environmental consequences.

Organic and synthetic gardening represent two different approaches to cultivation, differing in their growing styles, nutrient sources, and environmental impacts. By utilizing organic gardening practices, you are promoting environmental sustainability, reducing pollution, and supporting biodiversity. Additionally, by prioritizing soil health, organic gardening enhances the long-term fertility of the soil, resulting in healthier plants, and reduced reliance on external resources.

CHAPTER 2: ESSENTIAL ELEMENTS

ESSENTIAL *Elements*

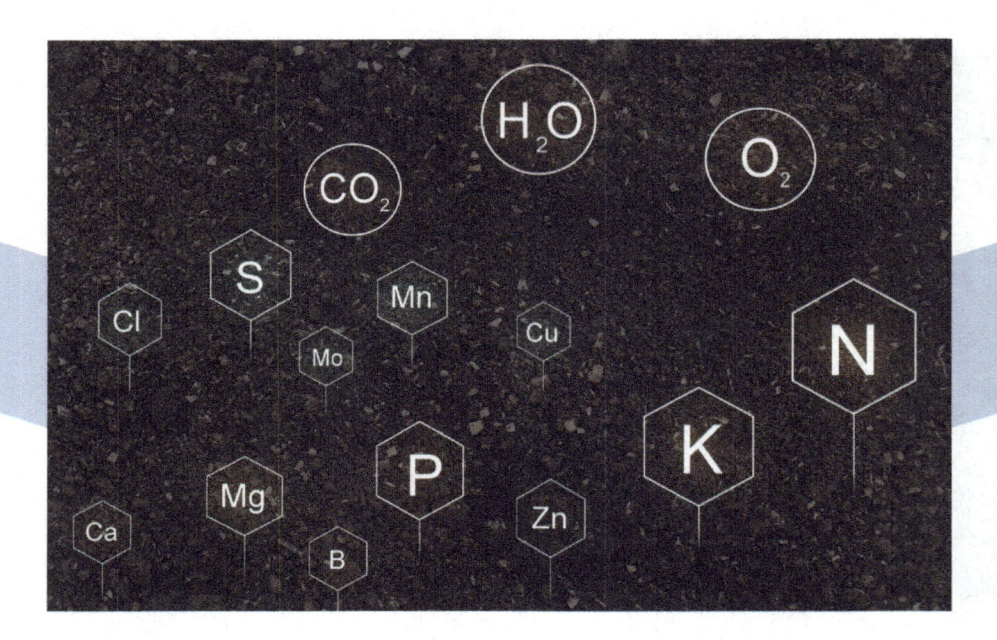

To ensure the healthy growth of a cannabis plant without nutrient deficiencies or toxicities, the grower must provide the plant with sufficient amounts of 17 essential elements. These elements are crucial for the plants' survival and overall health. While there are additional elements that contribute to growth and yield such as silicon (Si) and cobalt (Co), they are considered non-essential elements rather than essential.

The 17 essential elements consist of both mineral and non-mineral components. Non-mineral elements, such as oxygen (O) and carbon (C), are primarily acquired from the air through processes like photosynthesis. Hydrogen (H), on the other hand, is obtained from water absorbed by the plant roots in the growing medium.

Mineral elements are present and also added to the growing medium throughout the grow cycle. These mineral elements can be further categorized as macronutrients and micronutrients. The term "macronutrients" indicates that the plant requires them in larger quantities as they are critical for their survival. Micronutrients, on the other hand, are needed in smaller amounts. Despite their lower requirement, the absence of any of these essential micronutrients can severely damage a plant's health and stunt its growth, ultimately impacting overall yield.

MACRONUTRIENTS

Macronutrients are essential elements required in large amounts. They play a vital role in supporting the overall growth and development of the plant. The essential macronutrients for cannabis plants are as follows:

- **Nitrogen:** Nitrogen is essential for chlorophyll production, which is necessary for photosynthesis, protein synthesis, and plant growth.

- **Phosphorus:** Phosphorus plays a crucial role in overall plant growth, particularly during the flowering stage, bud production, and seedling stage. It also contributes to stem growth and strength.

- **Potassium:** Potassium facilitates nutrient and water movement within plants. It is essential for water uptake from roots and the absorption of other key nutrients.

- **Calcium:** Calcium is an immobile macronutrient that strengthens cell membranes and walls, protecting cannabis plants from diseases.

- **Magnesium:** Magnesium is vital for photosynthesis and enzyme production. Its deficiency can result in weak plants with stunted growth.

- **Sulfur:** Sulfur is important for chlorophyll formation, amino acid and protein production, and aids in the absorption of nitrogen.

MICRONUTRIENTS

Micronutrients are essential elements required in small amounts. It is important to note that their significance should not be underestimated simply due to their lower quantity requirements. The absence of any of these micronutrients can result in stunted growth, reduced yields, and poor health. The essential micronutrients for cannabis plants are as follows:

- **Boron:** Boron promotes tissue growth and enhances the absorption of macronutrients like calcium and magnesium. It also plays a role in flower formation and regulates plant metabolism.

- **Chlorine:** Chlorine is necessary for the hydrolysis process during photosynthesis and, in conjunction with potassium, regulates stomata opening.

- **Copper:** Copper is crucial for plant metabolism, including the metabolization of carbohydrates and proteins.

- **Iron:** Iron is required in trace amounts for protein synthesis and is an essential component for chlorophyll production.

- **Manganese:** Manganese is an essential micronutrient for supporting reproductive processes in plants, including pollen germination.

- **Molybdenum:** Molybdenum is necessary for the production of two enzymes that convert nitrate to nitrite.

- **Zinc:** Zinc is important for hormone production, which is responsible for internode elongation or stem growth.

- **Nickel:** Nickel is another important mineral that supports enzyme activity and metabolic processes.

The 17 essential elements that we have just covered certainly have additional roles within the plant beyond the ones mentioned. This overview simply provides a brief summary of the essential nutrients and highlights some of their major or commonly observed functions. By understanding the role of macro and micronutrients, you can address potential deficiencies and optimize plant health. Neglecting these essential elements can result in poor growth and diminished yields. Now that you have a clear understanding of the nutrients required for cannabis plant growth, let's continue on and discuss the tools and equipment you can utilize to ensure proper nutrient absorption and promote healthy growth.

CHAPTER 3: EQUIPMENT CHECKLIST

EQUIPMENT *Checklist*

Before you get started growing cannabis, it is crucial to ensure that you have the necessary tools and equipment available. Whether you choose to cultivate indoors or outdoors, the right tools and equipment will greatly contribute to your success. In this chapter, we will briefly outline some essential tools and equipment that will help you achieve a successful organic grow. While there are numerous tools available that can enhance quality and yield, it is important to prioritize the essentials. In this chapter, there are checklists of items to help you get started with organic cannabis cultivation.

Outdoor Tools & Equipment:

If you're growing cannabis outdoors, it doesn't require as many tools and equipment as indoor cultivation since you won't have full control over environmental conditions such as temperature, humidity, CO2 levels, and air circulation. Here is a list of recommended tools and equipment for outdoor growing:

- **Growing medium:** Choose between in-ground cultivation (if your soil is suitable) or purchase a soil or potting mix. Avoid inert mediums and hydroponic systems.

- **Containers:** Growers generally find it easier to grow in larger containers. More on this in the Containers chapter of this book.

- **Fertilizer:** Use an organic fertilizer blend or individual organic amendments to provide essential nutrients. Refer to the Base Inputs chapter for more information.

- **Pest prevention sprays:** Outdoor pest management differs from indoor cultivation. Explore strategies and products specific to outdoor pest prevention in the Pest Prevention chapter.

- **Sprayer:** Invest in a sprayer to apply organic pesticides and fertilizers effectively.

- **Watering hose or irrigation system:** Ensure you have the necessary equipment to water your plants as required. Check the Water chapter for further guidance.

- **Trimmers/shears:** Use a small pair of hand trimmers for pruning, or opt for shears when dealing with larger plants and branches.

Indoor Tools & Equipment:

Indoor cannabis cultivation requires additional equipment to maintain optimal environmental conditions. Here is a list of recommended tools and equipment for indoor growing:

- **Grow light(s):** Choose from LED, HPS, MH, or CMH lights, depending on your specific needs. Refer to the Lighting chapter for more details.

- **Grow light timer:** Use a timer to schedule the on/off cycle of your grow lights, unless your lights have a built-in timer.

- **Grow tent:** Consider using a grow tent to create a controlled environment, although it is optional.

- **Growing medium:** Use a soil or potting mix for organic indoor cultivation. Avoid inert mediums and hydroponic systems. More on this in the Soil chapter of this book.

- **Containers:** Opt for larger containers for ease of growing. Further information can be found in the Containers chapter.

- **Fertilizer:** Utilize an organic fertilizer blend or individual organic amendments for nutrient supply. Consult the Fertilizer chapter for detailed insights.

- **Ventilation system (inline fan, ducting, carbon filter):** Set up an effective ventilation system for air exchange. A carbon filter is optional if odor control is not a concern.

- **Oscillating fan:** Ensure proper air circulation to prevent hot spots and maintain CO2 contact with the leaves.

- **Temperature & humidity monitor:** Use a monitor to keep track of temperature and humidity levels within the grow space.

- **Watering can or automatic watering system:** Choose between manual watering using a watering can or container, or opt for an automatic watering system for more convenient watering.

- **Trimmers/shears:** Have a small pair of hand trimmers for pruning. For larger plants, shears are recommended for easier cutting.

Other Indoor Tools & Equipment:

Additional equipment may be necessary depending on factors like natural temperature and humidity, water source, and pest pressure. Consider the following tools and equipment:

- **Humidifier:** If humidity is too low, a humidifier can help increase it within the grow space.

- **Dehumidifier:** If humidity is too high, a dehumidifier can help reduce it within the grow space.

- **Heater:** Use a heater if temperatures are too low to maintain within the ideal range.

- **Air conditioner:** Employ an air conditioner if temperatures are too high and need to be lowered.

- **RO system:** If your water source is inadequate for healthy plant growth, consider a reverse osmosis (RO) system. Refer to the Water chapter for more information.

- **Yellow stickies:** Use yellow sticky traps to identify and monitor pests.

- **Pest prevention sprays:** Optional for indoor cultivation, depending on pest presence. Further guidance is available in the Pest Prevention chapter.

- **Sprayer:** Use a sprayer to apply organic pesticides and fertilizers effectively.

Other Common Tools & Equipment:

Here are some additional tools commonly used in cannabis cultivation:

- **Garden tool set (trowel, transplanter, and cultivator):** Facilitates digging and surface scratching during fertilizer application.

- **Bucket:** A 5-gallon bucket is useful for mixing water with microbial inoculants. Refer to the Microbes chapter for more details.

- **pH meter:** While not essential for organic growing, a pH meter can help troubleshoot plant deficiencies by measuring pH levels.

- **TDS Tester:** This tool provides a general idea of nutrient availability in the medium, even though it's not commonly used with organic inputs.

- **Trellis net:** Used for plant training and support.

- **Plant ties:** Useful for low-stress training of plants.

- **Plant clips:** Used to support branches or for low-stress training techniques.

- **Plant tags:** Labels for identifying plants.

- **Gloves:** Protect your hands when working in the garden.

Note: There is a wide range of tools and equipment available for cannabis cultivation, and the above list covers the basics considered essential. For a comprehensive list of recommended gardening tools and equipment, visit my website at www.mrgrowit.com.

Now that you are familiar with the essential tools and equipment required for successful cannabis cultivation, both indoors and outdoors, let's continue onto the following chapters, which cover crucial aspects such as soil, containers, and base inputs in greater detail.

CHAPTER 4: SOIL

SOIL

Now it's time to get into the meat and potatoes of organic gardening, starting with the foundation - the soil. Soil is defined as a mixture of organic matter, minerals, gases, liquids, and organisms that together support the life of plants and soil organisms. You may have also heard people refer to it as topsoil, potting soil, or a potting mix. In general, topsoil is for planting in the ground, while potting soil and potting mix are for planting in containers. Topsoil is a combination of sand or clay (ground-up rocks) mixed with organic materials such as compost. It is typically not ideal for growing cannabis since it does not provide much aeration. Potting soil is a mixture of peat moss and other organic materials such as perlite, vermiculite, compost, and worm castings. Other ingredients might include coconut coir, pit moss, and even fertilizer. Specific mixtures vary, depending on the use.

Choosing the best organic soil for your cannabis plants is arguably one of the most important decisions in an organic grow. It has a significant impact on the plant's growth rate and overall health. If a grower decides to grow in soil, it is crucial to be aware of the soil requirements for cannabis plants, as a lot is on the line, including the quality of the yield. Here are a few characteristics to look for in soil that you'll use for growing cannabis plants:

1. **Texture:** The texture of the soil refers to the relative proportions of different particle sizes found within the soil. These particles can be categorized into three main types: sand, silt, and clay. It is important to pick soil with a loose texture as it gives the cannabis plant's roots the ability to intake oxygen. Yes, plants do intake oxygen down in the root zone. Having a loose texture also helps ensure water movement and the ability to withhold nutrients; therefore, it is an important factor to consider.

2. **Drainage and Water Retention:** Good soil should have a balance between drainage and water retention. It should allow excess water to drain away to prevent waterlogging while still retaining enough moisture to sustain plant growth during dry periods.

3. **Nutrients:** The soil is the main source of nutrient absorption for cannabis plants. We covered the essential nutrients that the plant requires for growing back in chapter 2. Assess the soil's nutrient content, both macronutrients and micronutrients. A fertile soil with a good nutrient balance is important to ensure that the soil can provide all essential nutrients for the cannabis plant to support vigorous plant growth and healthy development.

4. **pH Level:** The soil's pH level is a measure of its acidity or alkalinity. Different plants have specific pH preferences, so it's essential to check whether the soil pH matches the requirements of the plants you intend to grow. Cannabis plants thrive in slightly acidic soil between 5.8 and 6.3 pH. Although cannabis can grow in soil that has a pH outside of that range, so don't feel like you must find soil in that pH range to complete a grow cycle successfully.

There are numerous options available when it comes to picking the right soil for cannabis plants, but with this information, it becomes easier to pick a good one. Bagged potting soil, super soil, and creating a custom mix are a couple of common options that you may consider.

BAGGED POTTING SOIL

Purchasing bagged potting soil from the store is a very convenient option. Since there are a lot of bagged soil options available nowadays, it is possible to find soil with the right texture, nutrient content, water retention qualities, and required pH levels. But without the right knowledge, it is also possible to pick a bag of potting soil that is not ideal for cannabis plants. Since many bagged potting soils usually go through a sterilization process, it is safe to state that it is mostly free of pests or diseases that may harm your cannabis plants.

The catch with this option is that the grower needs to know exactly what is required. These bags can also be expensive, and therefore, this is not always a wallet-friendly option. Additionally, storing the closed bags for more than a year is generally not recommended since the soil quality can deplete over time. Open bags should ideally be used within a few months of opening to ensure sufficient moisture and adequate nutrition.

SUPER SOIL

Super soil is a highly enriched and pre-amended type of soil mix. It is designed to provide all the essential nutrients and microbial life needed for your cannabis plants to thrive throughout their entire lifecycle, without the need to add any additional fertilizers throughout the grow cycle.

Super soil recipes vary, but they generally consist of a combination of high-quality organic ingredients, including but not limited to:

- **Base Soil:** A high-quality organic soil mix serves as the foundation of super soil. It is often a mix of compost, peat moss, coco coir, or other organic materials.

- **Amendments:** Super soil is heavily amended with various organic materials to provide a wide range of nutrients. Common amendments include bat guano, bone meal, blood meal, fish meal, kelp meal, and rock phosphate, among others. These amendments gradually release nutrients over time, ensuring a consistent supply for plant growth.

- **Microbial Life:** Beneficial microorganisms, like mycorrhizal fungi and beneficial bacteria, are essential components of super soil. They work symbiotically with plant roots, enhancing nutrient uptake and supporting plant health.

- **Minerals and Trace Elements:** Super soil may also include mineral-rich substances like azomite or glacial rock dust to provide essential trace elements and improve mineral content.

- **pH Balancing:** Some super soil recipes may incorporate ingredients to help balance the soil's pH and maintain it in the ideal range for cannabis plant growth.

The concept behind super soil is to create a living ecosystem within the soil that supports the natural processes of nutrient cycling and provides a stable and sustainable environment for plants. Once the super soil mix is prepared, it needs to "cook" or mature for several weeks or even months to allow the beneficial microbial activity to establish and the nutrients to become available for plants.

Super soil is popular among organic growers because it eliminates the need to add fertilizer throughout the grow cycle and minimizes the risk of nutrient deficiencies or toxicities. However, creating super soil can be more labor-intensive and may require a higher initial investment compared to simply buying a bagged potting mix from your local hydroponic store.

CUSTOM MIX

Many growers create their own custom soil mix. This option generally isn't recommended for beginners since an imbalance of nutrients in the soil can result in nutrient lockout and plant deficiencies. Although, with some time dedicated to research, you can devise your own mix for your plants to thrive in. One of the most common custom mixes among cannabis growers is the 1:1:1 mix. Simply put, the soil consists of three equal parts. One part of either peat moss or coco coir, one part aeration such as perlite, vermiculite, lava rock, or rice hulls, and one part compost or worm castings. Many growers will also add in fertilizer as well to ensure sufficient nutrition for the plants. This mix allows flexibility. You can alter the inputs and still achieve a good mix for growing cannabis plants in. We get into more details on this specific mix and another good soil recipe for growing cannabis in later on in this book.

NATIVE SOIL

Growing cannabis in the soil in your backyard (native soil) is a sustainable approach to growing your cannabis plants. Before getting started, it's highly recommended to get a soil test to understand its pH level, nutrient content, and overall texture. Based on the soil test results, consider amending the soil with organic matter, such as compost, to improve its fertility and structure. Native soils often provide a variety of natural nutrients, which can reduce the need to purchase additional organic amendments. Remember to check for proper drainage and water retention capabilities. You may need to add in an aeration amendment. You can also utilize mulching techniques to conserve moisture. We will cover mulching in detail in the Mulch chapter of this book.

Throughout this chapter, we have explored the fundamental principles of soil selection, soil mixing, and using the native soil in your backyard. There is certainly more that can be said about growing cannabis in soil and the topics we just covered. This knowledge should serve as a foundation that you can continuously build upon as you continue your journey of growing cannabis organically. Now, let's continue on to another essential topic when growing organic cannabis: choosing the right container.

CHAPTER 5: CONTAINERS

CONTAINERS

One of the most overlooked aspects of growing cannabis is the size and type of the grow pot or container. Depending on the container size you choose, growing cannabis can either become a challenge or be made easier. While it might not seem like selecting the right container type and size would make a significant difference, it actually does.

If you choose a container that is too small, the nutrients in the medium will quickly deplete, leading to deficiencies in the plant. Additionally, you'll find yourself spending more time watering the plant, as the roots will absorb the water in a smaller container faster than in a larger one.

On the other hand, choosing a container that is too big can also be problematic. If you accidentally add too much water to the medium, causing it to become excessively moist, the plant may be deprived of oxygen in the root zone, resulting in stunted growth. Additionally, with a large container relative to the plant's size and root zone, it may take a while for the medium to dry to the ideal moisture level and for the plant to recover.

In short, picking the right container can save you a lot of time and energy, while also contributing to the root growth and overall health of your cannabis plants. Whether you are growing indoors or outdoors, there are several options available for selecting containers that suit your needs. Here are a few options to consider:

PLASTIC POTS

Plastic pots are a popular and cost-effective option for growing cannabis organically. They come in various sizes, shapes, and colors, offering versatility for different plant needs. Pros include affordability, easy handling, good drainage, and reusability. Additionally, the medium will naturally dry out from the top down, mirroring how it occurs in nature. However, plastic pots may retain more heat, lack breathability, and can potentially lead to the plant becoming root bound. Root bound is when a plant's roots outgrow their container, hindering growth and nutrient absorption. Despite these drawbacks, plastic containers remain a viable choice for organic cannabis cultivation.

CLAY POTS

Clay pots, also known as terra cotta pots, are containers made from natural clay material. They have been used for centuries in gardening due to their unique properties and aesthetics. Clay pots offer breathability, temperature regulation, and eco-friendliness. The downsides are that they are susceptible to cracking, heavy, and their porous nature can lead to faster water evaporation, requiring more frequent watering. Due to this, clay pots are not commonly used for organic cannabis cultivation. Instead, alternative containers like plastic or fabric pots provide better control for achieving successful plant growth.

FABRIC POTS

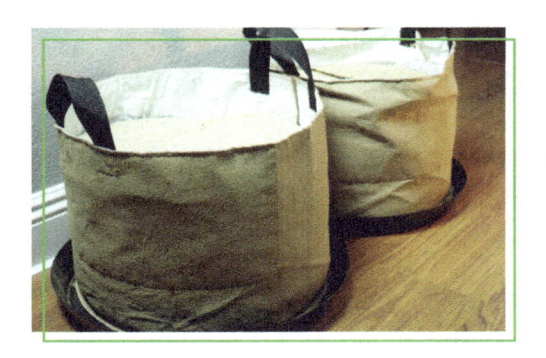

Fabric pots are breathable containers made of porous fabric. They have gained popularity among cannabis growers due to their unique design and advantages, including improved root health through air pruning, excellent drainage, and temperature regulation. They are lightweight and easy to move, but they may have a shorter lifespan and be slightly more expensive than plastic pots. Additionally, the medium dries out from all sides, which isn't natural and may cause a lack of nutrition in organic growing where consistent moisture is vital for proper amendment breakdown. Despite this, many organic growers still use fabric pots with success.

AIR POTS

Air pots, also known as air-pruning pots, feature openings along the sides for enhanced aeration and root pruning. Each root is guided by the shape of the pot wall towards an air hole, where the air dehydrates the root tip, leading to pruning and stimulating root branching. This process continues until a mass of healthy fibrous roots is formed.

Other benefits of air pots include providing sufficient oxygen to the root zone, excellent drainage, reusability, and ease of up-potting plants due to the container's ability to come apart easily. However, air pots tend to be more expensive, can dry out faster, and may expose roots in hot conditions. While they are favored by some cannabis growers, they aren't commonly used among organic cannabis growers. This is mainly due to the medium drying out from all sides, similar to fabric pots. Consistent moisture is crucial for proper amendment breakdown.

RAISED BEDS

When it comes to moving and cleaning grow pots, it can become labor-intensive, especially with a large setup and numerous pots. Raised beds provide a solution to this issue. A raised bed is an elevated gardening area often constructed from wood or stone. Pros include improved drainage, better soil control, and enhanced root health due to ample space for natural growth. However, setup effort and potential water requirements are drawbacks. Additionally, relocating raised beds can be challenging; if you want to shift the bed to a different area, it can require some serious effort, depending on the size of the bed. Raised beds are more common in outdoor cannabis cultivation due to the previously mentioned advantages and the lack of necessity to move the bed.

IN-GROUND

When growing outdoors, the simplest method is to plant directly in the ground. This involves sowing cannabis seeds or seedlings directly into the native soil without using containers. The benefits include exposing the plant to indigenous microorganisms and allowing the roots to naturally spread without confinement. Additionally, it eliminates the need to purchase grow pots, resulting in cost savings. However, there are downsides, including limited control over soil quality, which can lead to issues like soil compaction, poor drainage, and inadequate oxygen for the root zone, all of which can significantly hinder cannabis plant growth. Another concern is heavy metals. Cannabis is a bioaccumulator, meaning it can accumulate substances, including but not limited to contaminants like lead, cadmium, and arsenic, from the soil over time. This could pose a risk to human health if consumed. Therefore, it's generally advised to conduct a soil test before planting to check for heavy metal presence and determine the available nutrients. This information is also helpful for determining what soil amendments should be added for proper cannabis plant health.

CONTAINER SIZE

Container size is of utmost importance when growing cannabis organically because it directly impacts the plant's health and overall growth. Many organic cultivators opt for a larger container size, such as a 7 or 10-gallon grow pot at the minimum, while some growers prefer 15 or even 20-gallon containers as the minimum for organic cultivation. Growing in a larger container guarantees ample space for the root system to spread and access essential nutrients from the medium. It also provides a larger buffer and more room for organic amendments to be added throughout the grow cycle.

Some growers choose to start their seeds in smaller containers and then transplant them to larger ones just before the plants become root-bound. For instance, they may begin with a small 12-18 oz plastic cup and then transplant to a 7 or 10-gallon container 10-14 days after the plant sprouts from the soil. This approach has several benefits, such as conserving space initially, using a smaller grow light with less energy consumption, and allowing for the direct application of mycorrhizal fungi to the roots during transplanting. However, planting directly into a larger container for the plant's entire life is also a valid method.

If a plant is confined to a container that is too small, it may experience root binding and restricted growth, resulting in poor nutrient absorption and deficiencies. Additionally, an excessively large container can pose problems during watering, potentially causing oxygen deprivation in the root zone and stunted growth. The medium may also retain excessive moisture, potentially leading to root rot and hindering nutrient availability. By carefully selecting the appropriate container size, organic cannabis growers can create an ideal foundation for their plants, promoting healthy growth and maximizing the benefits of organic cultivation practices.

SAUCER VS TRAY

A plant saucer and a plant tray are both essential tools in gardening for managing excess water runoff and maintaining a clean growing area. A plant saucer is a shallow, circular dish placed under a potted plant to catch water draining from the bottom of the container, preventing water from seeping onto surfaces and protecting floors from potential water damage. It is ideal for individual pots and offers simplicity and space-saving benefits. Pros of using a plant saucer include easy handling, affordability, and the ability to be used multiple times. However, monitoring for accumulated water is necessary to avoid overwatering or standing water issues.

On the other hand, a plant tray is a larger, shallow container designed to hold multiple pots, efficiently collecting excess water from various plants. It is beneficial for gardeners dealing with several plants, simplifying watering routines and protecting surfaces from water damage. However, plant trays may require more space, and standing water in the tray could lead to overwatering if not closely monitored.

CHAPTER 6: BASE INPUTS

BASE *Inputs*

Now, we come to one of the most crucial processes in cannabis cultivation - providing the plant with the necessary nutrition. In informal conversations, some might mention they "feed their plant" and then list a lineup of bottled products, usually synthetic fertilizers. In that case, saying "feeding the plant" is accurate, as the nutrients in these bottles are readily absorbable by the plant. However, if someone were to say they are "feeding their plant" and then mention an organic fertilizer or amendment, it wouldn't be correct. Most organic inputs are not in a form the plant can immediately utilize; they first need to be broken down by microorganisms and converted into a plant-absorbable form. In essence, you're not feeding the plant; you're actually feeding the soil.

With this in mind, let's explore various methods of feeding the soil with organic inputs. There's no one-size-fits-all approach; multiple methods and inputs are available for growing cannabis organically. This chapter will provide a detailed guide on using organic fertilizer blends throughout the grow cycle. Additionally, we'll touch upon using worm castings and compost which are organic inputs that can also be utilized to enhance soil nutrition. Keep in mind, if the plant doesn't receive the required nutrients for growth, it will show signs of deficiencies and experience stunted growth. Providing your plants with the proper nutrition will help ensure the plants are healthy and produce a good yield.

ORGANIC FERTILIZER BLENDS

Fertilizer blends, also known as fertilizer packs, are a mix of various organic and natural ingredients. These blends can contain components like fish meal, blood meal, oyster shells, kelp meal, and more. You can find a detailed list of ingredients on the package. Look for the N-P-K ratio (nitrogen-phosphorus-potassium) and a Guaranteed Analysis on the package. It's also important to check for heavy metal test results. If this information on where to access heavy metal test results isn't referenced on the package, be cautious. As mentioned in a previous chapter, cannabis can accumulate heavy metals that are harmful for human consumption. While many organic fertilizers contain essential elements categorized in the heavy metal category like copper, nickel, molybdenum, and zinc that are beneficial for cannabis, avoiding harmful heavy metals like arsenic, cadmium, and lead is crucial.

Once you've ensured that the organic fertilizer blend you plan to use both provides the required nutrition and is safe, the next step is understanding how to apply it correctly. The application rate varies depending on the specific blend you're using. Some blends only need a one-time application, while others require periodic reapplication. For instance, KIS Organics Nutrient Pack provides the instruction, "Apply 1 cup of nutrient pack per 10 gallons of soil in pots or 1/2 cup per square foot of outdoor soil." This is applied as a top-dressing, where you sprinkle the blend on the soil's surface and mix it into the top layer. Typically, this should be done every 30 days, but factors such as pot size and plant size can influence the frequency. There are alternative ways to use the blend, such as amending used soil or creating a "Water-Only Living Soil."

Another example is the Build-A-Soil Craft Blend. Its application instructions suggest that you can re-amend your used organic soil with 2-4 cups per cubic foot, top dress at 1/4 to 1 cup per plant, or make a tea with it by using 1/4 to 1 cup per 5-gallon bucket of water. This goes to show that there are several effective ways to use organic fertilizer blends.

Some of you may have experience with synthetic nutrients, where the general advice is to use only half or even a quarter of the recommended dose from the feeding chart. With organic fertilizer blends, it's best to follow the application instructions provided on the package.

Numerous companies manufacture organic fertilizer blends, too many to list here. However, some popular options include Down To Earth, Dr. Earth, and Mr. B's Green Trees. Regardless of the brand, always pay attention to the application rate specified on the package for the best results.

There are many more organic inputs that you can use in your garden such as alfalfa meal, fish meal, insect frass, and oyster shells, to name just a few. In a later chapter in this book, we'll explore 20 different organic fertilizers and amendments. You'll learn what each input is, how it benefits your garden, and its recommended application rate. We'll also cover how you can use these organic inputs to address nutrient deficiencies in your plants.

WORM CASTINGS

Worm castings, often referred to as "black gold," is a nutrient-rich organic fertilizer and one of the most commonly used organic inputs in gardening. Essentially, it is earthworm waste, and it's packed with beneficial microorganisms and essential nutrients such as nitrogen, phosphorus, potassium, and micronutrients. Additionally, worm castings contribute to improved soil structure and aeration - and this is just the tip of the iceberg when it comes to its benefits.

Worm castings can be safely incorporated into the soil throughout a plant's life cycle. They can be applied in various ways such as mixing into the soil before planting, top dressing, or as a component in compost tea. For an initial soil amendment, it's generally recommended to use 15-20% worm castings in your mix. When applying them as a top dressing, a 1-2-inch layer on top of the medium is often recommended. And for those brewing compost teas, a typical guideline is to use 2 cups of worm castings per 5 gallons of water.

By utilizing worm castings in your garden, you not only boost the population of beneficial microorganisms in your soil but also provide the essential nutrition your plants need. Many dedicated organic gardeners firmly believe that every organic gardener should make use of worm castings, as their benefits far outweigh those of other organic inputs.

COMPOST

Some gardeners rely solely on compost as their fertilizer. Compost is produced through the decomposition of organic materials like kitchen scraps, yard waste, and plant matter. It's a highly beneficial natural input that provides essential elements for cannabis plant growth. When you incorporate compost into the soil, it gradually breaks down over time. Compost not only supplies the essential nutrients that cannabis plants need but also brings beneficial microorganisms and serves as an excellent soil conditioner. Its organic matter improves soil structure, enhancing both water retention and drainage.

The recommended application rate can vary depending on the type of compost you have. As a general guideline, spreading a 1-3-inch layer over the soil's surface and mixing it with the 2-4-inch layer of soil below is advisable. It's crucial to avoid over-application, as excessive compost can lead to nutrient imbalances and hinder root growth. While some growers rely solely on compost and exclude other inputs, many recommend using compost in combination with other organic inputs or a fertilizer blend for optimal results.

Compost stands out as one of the best inputs for your garden because you can create it yourself, saving money on fertilizer purchases. Later in this book, we break down some of the composting processes into more detail.

CHAPTER 7: LIGHTING

LIGHTING

*L*ight plays a crucial role in the growth of cannabis. Without proper lighting, cannabis plants are unable to photosynthesize, resulting in unhealthy, stunted growth. This principle holds true whether you are growing your plants outdoors or indoors. In this chapter, we will cover essential information regarding outdoor and indoor lighting. We will also go over light cycles, various types of indoor grow lights, and the amount of light needed for optimal growth.

OUTDOORS

When growing cannabis outdoors, sunlight serves as the primary source of light. In general, there is typically enough sunlight to maintain photoperiod cannabis plants in the vegetative stage during the spring and a portion of the summer. However, as late summer transitions into fall, the duration of sunlight begins to diminish, triggering photoperiod cannabis plants to initiate the flowering stage. It's important to note that the timing of this transition can significantly vary depending on your specific geographical location. Auto-flowering cannabis cultivars, on the other hand, are less sensitive to light changes and automatically transition to flowering after a certain number of weeks.

During the daytime, it's crucial to ensure that your cannabis plants receive between 10 to 12 hours of direct sunlight for optimal growth. While cannabis can survive with as little as 6 hours of direct sunlight, such limited exposure often results in stunted growth and reduced yields.

INDOORS

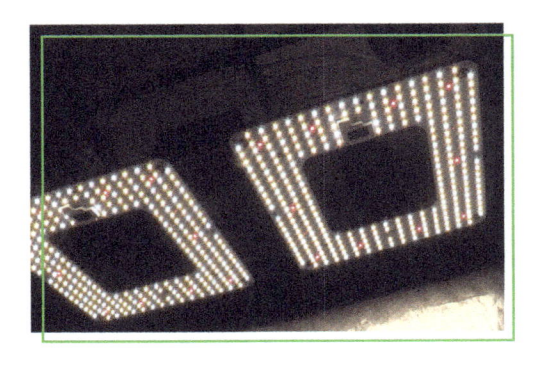

When growing cannabis indoors, a solid understanding of lighting provides greater control over the growing environment. Various types of grow lights are available for indoor cultivation, each offering distinct advantages and drawbacks. To make an informed choice, growers should understand the pros and cons of each lighting option.

- **LED Lights:** LED grow lights currently stand as the most popular choice for indoor cannabis cultivation due to their cost-effectiveness and energy efficiency. They also emit minimal heat.

- **HID Lights:** HID grow lights consist of metal halide, high-pressure sodium, and ceramic metal halide fixtures. While they can yield excellent results, they are less efficient when compared to LED grow lights and involve higher operational costs.

- **Fluorescent Lights:** Fluorescent lights are an economical option but typically deliver a smaller yield per watt compared to other lighting types. They are compact and unlikely to cause light burn, making them well-suited for small spaces, seedlings, and clones.

When determining the optimal amount of light required for successful cannabis growth, it's essential to consider environmental factors such as temperature, humidity, and CO2 levels, in addition to the specific cannabis cultivar you are growing. The most common measurement for light is PAR (Photosynthetically Active Radiation), which represents the light energy absorbed by your plants. Grow light listings often mention PAR output in terms of PPF (Photosynthetic Photon Flux) or PPFD (Photosynthetic Photon Flux Density):

- PPF quantifies the total light energy emitted by a grow light.

- PPFD gauges the amount of PAR reaching a specific area, typically one square meter, per second.

General guidelines for PPFD values during different growth stages are as follows:

- Seedlings, clones, and mother plants: 200-400 PPFD

- Vegetative stage: 400-600 PPFD

- Flowering stage: 600-900 PPFD

It's worth noting that under certain environmental conditions, you may be able to provide your plants with higher PAR levels, such as by supplementing the grow room with CO2, which will help your plants to absorb more PAR.

When selecting grow lights for your grow space, several other factors come into play, including coverage area, efficiency, cost, light spectrum, and more. Understanding the concept of PAR and adhering to general PAR recommendations for different growth stages ensures you choose an appropriate grow light for your space and helps you determine the optimal light distance to prevent issues like light stress and heat stress.

LIGHT CYCLE

Another essential factor to consider when it comes to lighting for growing cannabis indoors is the light cycle. The light cycle refers to the ratio of light-on to light-off time, and for photoperiod cannabis plants, it plays a pivotal role in their transition from the vegetative to the flowering stage. In the vegetative stage, the most common light cycle is 18/6, which means 18 hours of light and 6 hours of darkness. You can provide 24 hours of continuous light during this stage, although it tends to be costlier with few proven benefits.

During the flowering stage, the most common light cycle for photoperiod cannabis plants is 12/12, which is 12 hours of light and 12 hours of uninterrupted darkness. This light cycle artificially triggers the flowering process.

Auto-flowering plants, on the other hand, can remain on a vegetative light cycle throughout their entire life. They do not require a transition to a 12/12 light cycle to initiate flowering. However, it's worth noting that they can still be successfully grown under a 12/12 light cycle, although it may result in slower growth and a smaller yield.

With an understanding of some of the lighting requirements for cannabis plants in place, let's proceed to the next chapter, where we will cover environmental conditions in detail. This chapter will provide insights into other critical factors such as temperature, humidity, CO_2, and air circulation - all of which are essential for a successful grow.

CHAPTER 8: ENVIRONMENT

ENVIRONMENT

There are various environmental conditions that impact the way cannabis plants grow, including temperature, humidity, CO2, and air circulation. These factors can significantly affect both the yield and overall health of cannabis plants. When growing outdoors, you have limited control over these conditions. However, when growing indoors, you have a greater level of control and can maintain them within a specific range to promote optimal growth. In this chapter, we will discuss the key environmental factors of temperature, humidity, CO2 levels, and air circulation. A basic understanding of how to monitor and manage these conditions will help you successfully complete a grow cycle.

TEMPERATURE

The temperature in the grow environment can significantly impact plant growth. Generally, if the conditions in the grow room or outdoors make the grower uncomfortable, such as it being too hot or too cold, it's likely that the temperature isn't ideal for cannabis plants. Therefore, accurately measuring and monitoring the temperature is crucial. To do this, a grower should have a reliable thermometer. Maintaining the temperature within the ideal range in an indoor grow room can be achieved by using an air conditioner or a heater, depending on specific needs. It's important to note that using either an air conditioner or a heater can affect humidity levels in the grow room.

Cannabis plants thrive when the temperature falls within the range of 70-85°F (21-29°C) while the lights are on. To preserve terpenes, many growers slightly lower the grow room temperature during the final two weeks of the flowering stage to around 75-78°F (23-25°C). During the lights-off period, temperatures between 66-75°F (18-23°C) are ideal, as slight cooling doesn't significantly impact the plants. However, if it becomes too cold, it can cause stress, hinder growth, and even lead to overnight freezing damage. Keep in mind that this is a general temperature range, and cannabis plants can tolerate a wider range of conditions than their optimal range.

HUMIDITY

Another important parameter to monitor is the relative humidity (RH) level. To measure humidity in the grow room, you'll need a hygrometer. Humidifiers and dehumidifiers come in handy for regulating humidity levels in the grow room. It's important to note that using these devices can also influence the temperature, as these factors are interconnected. Temperature and humidity levels are interdependent when it comes to achieving optimal growth rates. Here are general relative humidity ranges that can promote healthy plant growth:

- Seedlings & Clones: 65 to 85% RH
- Vegetative stage: 45 to 70% RH
- Flowering stage: 40 to 60% RH

It's worth noting that these are general humidity ranges, and achieving optimal growth may involve monitoring and controlling the Vapor Pressure Deficit (VPD) instead. In simpler terms, VPD entails aiming for a specific humidity level based on the leaf surface temperature. You can find various VPD charts online that indicate the recommended humidity levels for different temperatures. Maintaining your grow room within the optimal VPD range helps ensure that the stomata on the leaves remain open, allowing for efficient photosynthesis. Many beginner growers may not prioritize staying within the ideal VPD range since it often requires higher humidity levels, which can lead to issues like powdery mildew and bud rot if there isn't sufficient air circulation in the grow environment.

CO2

One of the most effective ways to increase cannabis plant growth and yield is by introducing carbon dioxide (CO2) into the grow room. The target CO2 range is generally 800-1400 PPM (parts per million), and one study shows that CO2 levels at 1400 PPM led to an incredible 30% increase in yield! Raising CO2 levels in an indoor garden through organic methods can be achieved by providing a natural and chemical-free CO2 source. Here are a few organic approaches to boost CO2 levels in your indoor garden:

- **Composting:** Introducing compost into or near your indoor garden can effectively raise CO2 levels organically. As organic matter decomposes, it naturally generates CO2 as a byproduct.

- **Fermentation:** If you have any fermentation processes happening nearby, such as making homemade kombucha or beer, the CO2 released during fermentation can be used to enhance CO2 levels.

- **Mycorrhizal Fungi:** Mycorrhizal fungi establish symbiotic relationships with plant roots, improving nutrient uptake, water absorption, and even CO2 utilization. By encouraging the growth of these beneficial fungi in your soil, you indirectly help your plants access more CO2.

- **Exhaled Breath:** If you live in the same house where you're growing, or if you spend time in your indoor garden, your exhaled breath releases CO2. While this may have a minor effect on increasing CO2 levels, it's still worth mentioning.

- **Baking Soda and Vinegar Reaction:** A simple and organic method involves placing a container with baking soda (sodium bicarbonate) and another with vinegar (acetic acid) in your grow space. When these two substances react, they release CO2. However, this method may not offer a consistent and controllable source of CO2.

While these methods can help boost CO2 levels organically, it's important to understand that they may not provide the same precision and control over CO2 enrichment as traditional methods, such as using CO2 tanks or generators. Additionally, it's crucial to monitor CO2 levels to ensure they remain within the optimal range for plant growth, as excessive CO2 can be harmful.

AIR CIRCULATION

The last environmental factors we'll discuss are air circulation and exchange. In simple terms, it's crucial to ensure fresh air enters the grow space and that the air circulates continuously. This not only guarantees that plants have access to CO_2 but also reduces the risk of pests and prevents the development of hot and humid areas within the grow space.

To achieve effective air exchange, an inline fan and ducting are typically sufficient. The general rule of thumb is to exchange the air in the grow space every 1-5 minutes, depending on the plant size and the size of the grow area. For example, if you have four small seedlings in a 4'x4' grow tent, you won't need to exchange the air as frequently as you would with four large flowering plants in the same space.

Regarding air circulation, I recommend using at least two oscillating fans. Having two (or more) ensures that even if one malfunctions, there will be another fan to keep the air moving. This is essential for preventing issues like powdery mildew and bud rot, which can be a real headache. It's important that the air circulation provides a gentle breeze onto the plants rather than a direct, harsh blast of air, as this can lead to windburn.

Now that you have gained an understanding of the different environmental conditions and how to control them, you're prepared to continue to the next chapter, which submerges into the topic of water.

CHAPTER 9: WATER

WATER

The most sustainable approach to growing your plants involves making the most of your available water sources. Tap water, well water, rainwater, and reverse osmosis are all viable options in organic systems. However, it's important to be aware that certain elements present in these water sources, or an excess of certain elements, could potentially have adverse effects. Conducting water testing to identify harmful contaminants and understanding the ideal pH range can help you determine whether your water source is suitable for use in your organic system, and if necessary, how it can be treated. Once you confirm the suitability of your water source, mastering the techniques and timing of watering will contribute to the healthy growth of your plants at an accelerated pace.

WATER TESTING

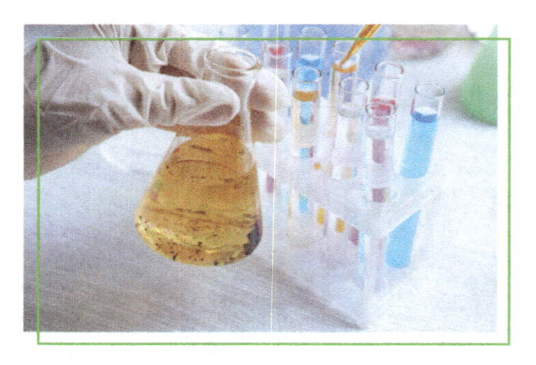

Your source of water could contain elements that your plant doesn't require. Heavy metals are a concern (as discussed in the Base Inputs chapter) and some elements may have a high presence which can actually prevent the plant from being able to absorb other elements. For example, an excess of sodium can reduce calcium and/or potassium absorption. This is just one example of a key nutrient relationship that can have an antagonistic effect - there are many more beyond that. Therefore, it's generally advisable to have your water tested so that you can determine what is in it and whether or not it is helpful or harmful to your plants.

If you live in the United States, Logan Labs is a popular choice for water testing. As of writing this book, they charge $35 for an "Irrigation Water Monitoring" package that includes results for: pH, soluble salts, chloride, bicarbonate, carbonate, alkalinity, hardness, SAR, calcium, magnesium, potassium, sodium, iron, boron and sulfate. They also have a package that will provide those results in addition to: nitrate, adjusted SAR, pHc, and phosphorus. If you're not sure how to read the results or what action to take afterwards, I recommend reaching out to the Soil Doctor, Bryant Mason. He is a Certified Crop Advisor (CCA) who specializes in organic soil and crop mineral nutrition. Basically he will read your test results and advise you on what action to take. This can be extremely valuable and ease your mind in knowing that your water source can be used without harmful or adverse effects.

CHLORINE & CHLORAMINE

Another consideration is the presence of chlorine and chloramine. These chemicals are sometimes added by local water municipalities to eliminate microorganisms, both beneficial and harmful ones, from the water supply. To identify whether your local water contains these chemicals, you should be able to review the water report provided by your town or city. Taking steps to reduce and/or eliminate these elements will help ensure the microorganisms in your medium aren't harmed so they can do their job of breaking down the organic inputs converting them to a form that your plant can then uptake.

If your water contains chlorine (and not chloramine), you can simply let the water sit out for 24 to 48 hours to let the chlorine dissipate. Exposure to light during this period can expedite the dissipation process. There are also various products out there that will neutralize and assist in the reduction of contaminants, including chlorine. Although, letting the water sit for a day or two doesn't cost any money so most prefer to do that. It is worth noting that some growers skip this step and directly water their plants with chlorinated tap water - and their plants still thrive. Think about all the gardeners who use a hose to water their plants in the backyard – their plants don't die off after watering, do they? Nope. However, the negative impact of chlorinated water on soil microorganisms is still there. As a precautionary measure, many growers prefer to let the chlorine dissipate, as I explained, before watering their plants.

On the other hand, chloramine doesn't dissipate like chlorine. Some gardeners still use water treated with chloramine to irrigate their plants and will get to harvest. However, just like chlorine, this may harm the microbial life in the soil. To mitigate this, most gardeners will take one of the following steps to remove chloramine from the water:

- **Dechlorination Tablets or Solutions:** You can find dechlorination tablets or liquid solutions at gardening stores or aquarium supply shops. These products are designed to remove chlorine and chloramine from tap water.

- **Activated Carbon Filters:** Activated carbon filters, often found in water filter pitchers or under-sink filtration systems, can help remove chloramine. Make sure the filter you use is specifically designed to handle chloramine removal, as not all activated carbon filters are equally effective in this regard.

- **Reverse Osmosis (RO) Filtration:** RO filtration systems can remove chloramine, along with many other contaminants, from water. These systems are typically installed under the sink or at the point of entry for your water supply.

There are other methods out there to remove chloramine from water; the three methods above are just the most common methods. Before choosing a method for chloramine removal, it's important to consider factors like the volume of water you need to treat and the ongoing maintenance associated with each method. If you are unsure about which method to use or need to treat a large volume of water, consulting with a water treatment specialist or a local water quality authority can be helpful.

PH

PH levels also play a vital role in water management for organic gardeners. In the gardening community, there's an ongoing debate about whether adjusting the pH of water before using it on the soil is necessary to ensure optimal nutrient absorption. Some gardeners opt for pH adjustments, while others don't, and their plants still thrive.

Several factors affect pH levels within the growing medium, including the activity of microorganisms and the release of acids by plants. The primary microorganisms that work closely with plants can handle pH levels ranging from 5.0 to 7.0. These microorganisms break down organic matter and trade the resulting nutrients for exudates released by plants into the root zone. Additionally, plants themselves release acids into the root zone, which naturally lowers the pH level. This acidification process is especially critical for elements like iron, which becomes more accessible when the pH is below 6.5. However, it's worth noting that some gardeners claim success with pH levels as high as 8.0. Regardless of your choice of pH for watering your plants, it's essential to weigh the potential pros and cons.

HOW TO WATER

You could have an excellent water source with a sufficient amount of essential nutrients within the ideal pH range, but if you don't apply the water to the soil properly, your plant may suffer. Knowing when and how much to water is crucial for successful organic cannabis cultivation.

Watering practices vary significantly between organic and synthetic cultivation methods. In my beginner's guide to growing cannabis, I discussed the practice of watering until runoff and allowing the growing medium to dry out between watering sessions, specifically when using synthetic bottled nutrients. This method serves several purposes, including reducing pest pressure (in particular, pests that thrive in moist environments) and implementing drought stress to stimulate secondary metabolite production.

In organic cultivation, microorganisms need to break down organic inputs into forms the plant can absorb. Maintaining a consistently moist medium keeps these microorganisms active, as they become dormant when the medium dries out. Active microorganisms efficiently break down nutrients for plant uptake. However, maintaining the right moisture level without overwatering and depriving the roots of oxygen can be challenging. Therefore, it's crucial to begin with well-aerated potting soil (as discussed in the Soil chapter) to ensure both oxygen availability within the root zone and the ideal moisture level.

You have several options for watering your plants. The most common method is hand watering using a container like a bucket or pitcher. Automated watering systems, such as Blumat carrots (my personal favorite choice), or drip systems, are also suitable for use with organic living soil. Additionally, a handheld sprayer on a wand can be helpful for reaching plants that are difficult to access. You can choose any of these methods based on your preference.

The next question is, how much water should you apply and when? This is a common question among new organic cannabis growers and can be challenging to answer. Factors like the plant's container size, the moisture level of the medium before watering, and the plant's size all come into play when determining the amount of water to apply to the soil. For instance, a large plant in a small container with dry soil may require more water than a small plant in a large container with pre-moistened soil. As you can see, there's no one-size-fits-all answer to the question of "how much water." This is where having a moisture meter can be helpful, taking the guesswork out of the equation.

Moisture meters, also known as soil moisture sensors, are tools that many gardeners overlook despite their significant benefits. These devices function by measuring the moisture content in the soil around your plants' roots, enabling precise watering. To use one, simply insert the meter's probe into the soil near your plant's roots. The meter operates on the principle of electrical conductivity: dry soil has higher resistance, while wet soil has lower resistance. As a result, the meter provides a reading, displaying soil moisture as a numeric value or visual indicator. Using a moisture meter eliminates guesswork in watering, resulting in healthier plants and resource conservation.

If you don't have a moisture meter, you might consider using the 5% rule. This means adding 5% of the size of the grow pot as water. For instance, if the plant is in a 10-gallon container, add half a gallon of water, which equals 5% of the pot's size. This method helps prevent overwatering. Growers then rely on visual cues, like drooping or upright leaves 'praying' towards the light, or they may touch the soil or lift/tilt the grow pot to gauge moisture levels. For beginners, it can be challenging to pinpoint the right timing, but with some practice, mastering when and how much to water becomes easier.

CHAPTER 10: MICROBES

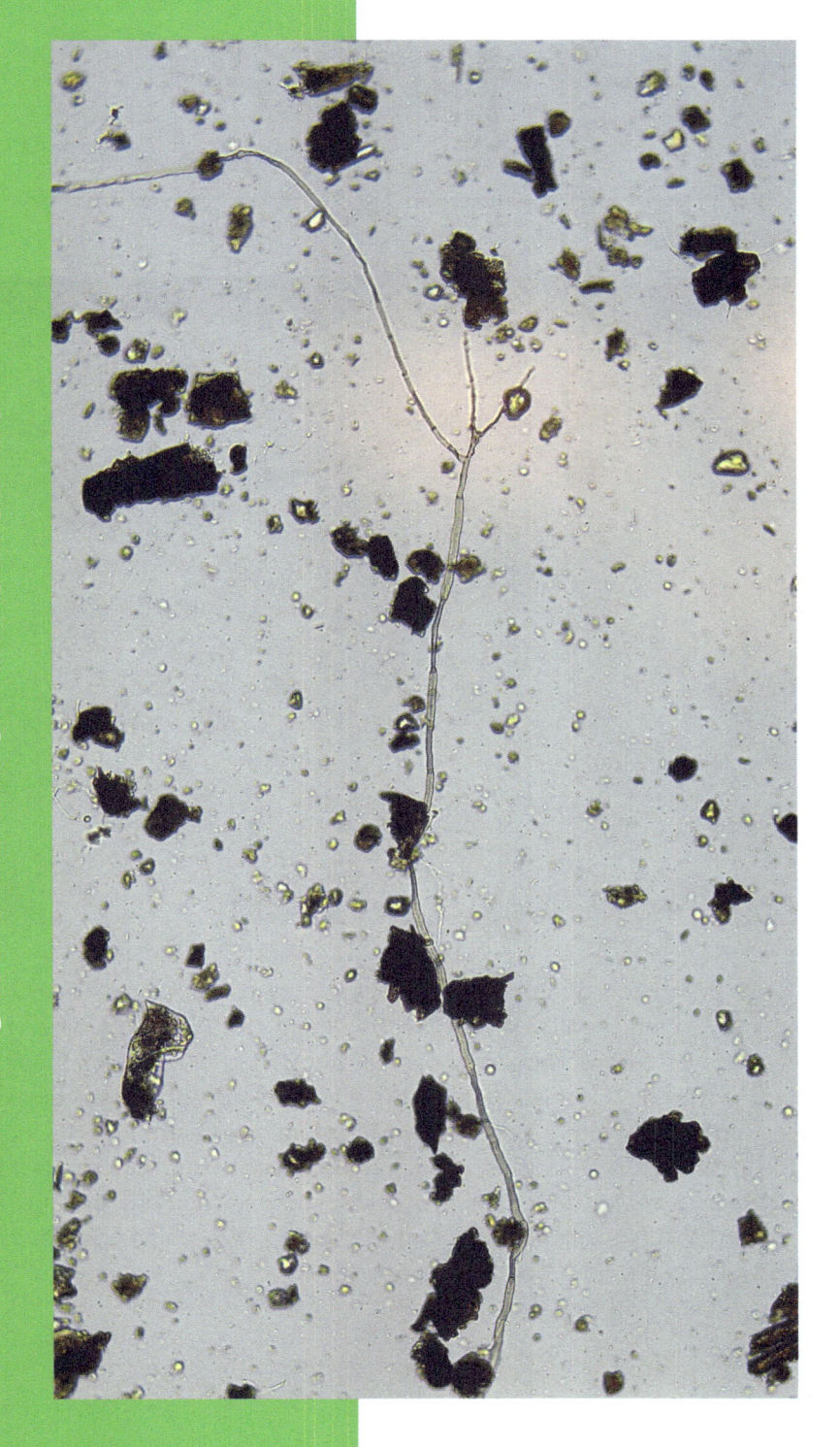

MICROBES

M Microorganisms (or microbes) play a crucial role in maintaining plant health. Within the soil, there are billions of different types of microorganisms, and a staggering 99.99% of them remain undiscovered. There is much we have yet to learn about soil biology, and our understanding is rapidly evolving. One well-established fact is that the network of organisms, including both micro and macro life forms, is indispensable for essential processes such as nutrient cycling, organic matter decomposition, and plant well-being. We commonly refer to this network as the Soil Food Web.

In this chapter, I will provide a high-level overview of what the Soil Food Web entails and how it functions. Additionally, we will explore the top five microorganisms in the soil food web: bacteria, archaea, fungi, protozoa, and nematodes. Lastly, we will dive into the advantages of using microbial inoculants and offer guidance on how to tap into their potential to improve soil and plant health.

THE SOIL FOOD WEB

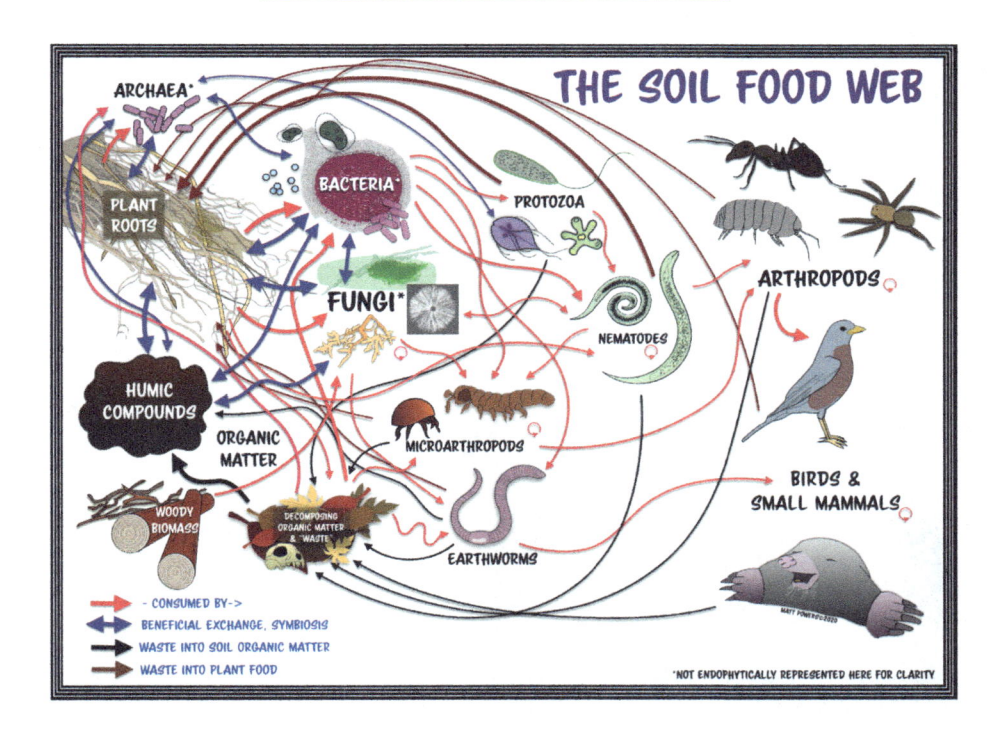

The Soil Food Web, in simple terms, is a living ecosystem within the Earth's soil. It's made up of a community of organisms that live either entirely or partially in the soil. These organisms interact with each other, and these interactions affect both plants and the overall health of the soil.

As plants grow, they release a variety of organic substances from their roots into the soil around them. We often call these substances "rhizodeposits," and they serve as food for microorganisms. Bacteria, fungi, protozoa, nematodes, and various other soil-dwelling creatures consume these substances, breaking them down into simpler compounds.

This initial transformation of organic matter starts an important process called "mineralization." During mineralization, important nutrients are released from the organic compounds. These nutrients become available for plants to absorb and use for their own growth and development. This creates a nutrient-rich environment where organisms not only compete for resources but also work together, forming partnerships that boost the soil's productivity.

Additionally, as microorganisms go about their metabolic processes, they produce byproducts that go back into the soil. These byproducts serve as essential building blocks for the soil's structure and composition. They help create stable soil aggregates, which improve the soil's ability to hold onto moisture and allow for better airflow. This creates an environment that's good for both microbes and healthy plant roots.

In the soil food web, each participant has a crucial role in maintaining a delicate balance. All of the interactions come together to create a soil environment that is not only fertile and full of nutrients but also rich in biological diversity.

BACTERIA

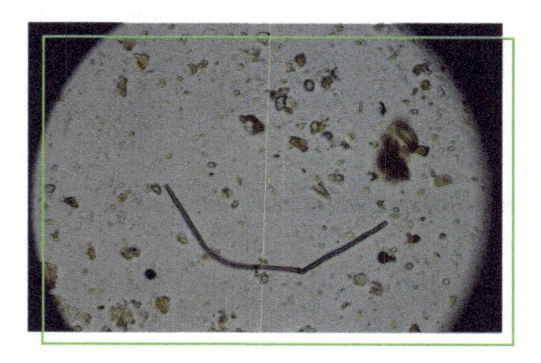

Bacteria are tiny, single-celled organisms abundant in soil, and they play a crucial role in maintaining soil health and fertility. These microscopic organisms break down organic matter within the soil, releasing essential nutrients such as nitrogen, phosphorus, and potassium in forms accessible to plants. It's important to note that the specific nutrients released can vary depending on the type of organic matter being decomposed and the bacterial species involved.

Bacteria also contribute to soil structure by producing substances that bind soil particles, enhancing moisture retention and erosion resistance. Additionally, they can suppress harmful pathogens through resource competition or by producing antimicrobial compounds, creating a disease-resistant environment for plants.

Some bacteria are nitrogen-fixers, capable of converting atmospheric nitrogen (which plants can't directly use) into a plant-friendly form. This process acts as a natural fertilizer for your garden, ensuring your plants receive an ample supply of this vital nutrient.

ARCHAEA

Archaea are a group of microorganisms that share similarities with bacteria but have distinct characteristics. While they may not be as widely recognized as bacteria, archaea play a vital role in soil ecosystems. These microorganisms are often referred to as extremophiles because they thrive in extreme conditions, such as high temperatures, high salinity, and acidic environments.

Archaea contribute to soil health in several ways. One of their essential roles is in nitrogen cycling. Just like certain bacteria, some archaea can convert atmospheric nitrogen into a form usable by plants, aiding in nitrogen fixation. Archaea also participate in the decomposition of organic matter, breaking down complex materials and facilitating nutrient release. Although archaea might be less well-known than other soil microorganisms, they are integral to creating a balanced and fertile soil environment that supports healthy plant growth.

FUNGI

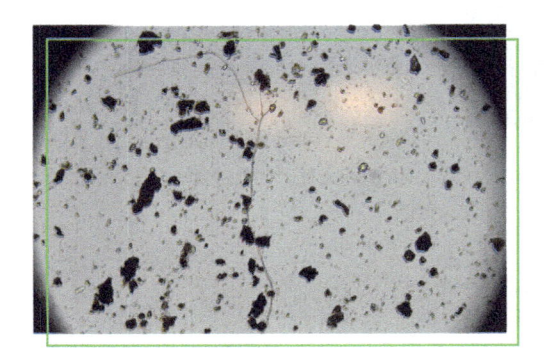

Fungi are a diverse group of microorganisms that offer significant benefits to your cannabis plants. They not only decompose organic matter like bacteria and archaea but also form symbiotic relationships with plants, notably mycorrhizal fungi. Essentially, fungi extend their thread-like structures, known as hyphae, into a plant's root system. In exchange, the plant provides the fungi with sugars produced through photosynthesis, creating a mutually beneficial partnership. This connection enhances a plant's capacity to absorb water and nutrients, particularly phosphorus, which can be scarce in many soils.

Fungi also greatly contribute to soil structure by establishing a network of hyphae that binds soil particles together, improving soil stability and water retention. Additionally, they play a role in disease suppression, as certain fungi can produce compounds that inhibit harmful pathogens, resulting in a healthier soil environment for your plants.

PROTOZOA

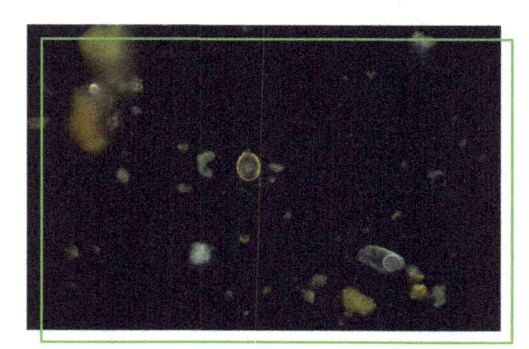

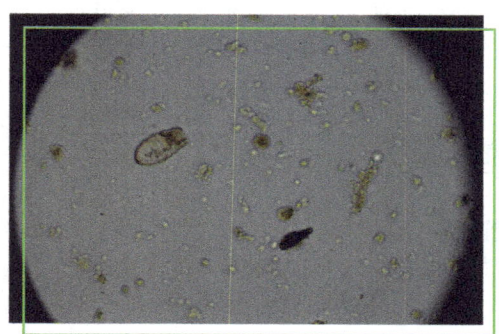

Protozoa are tiny, single-celled organisms that are primarily known as microbial predators. They feed on smaller microorganisms like bacteria and other protozoa. Their activities promote the development of beneficial microorganism communities and maintain a balanced soil ecosystem by helping regulate their populations. This has a positive impact on the composition of the soil microbiome and also indirectly affects nutrient cycling and mineralization processes. When protozoa consume bacteria, they release nutrients like nitrogen and phosphorus in a form that plants can more readily absorb, effectively acting as natural nutrient recyclers.

NEMATODES

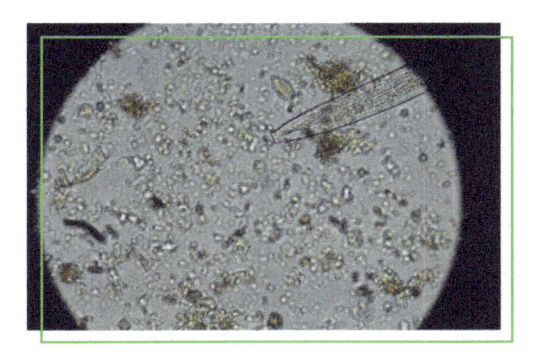

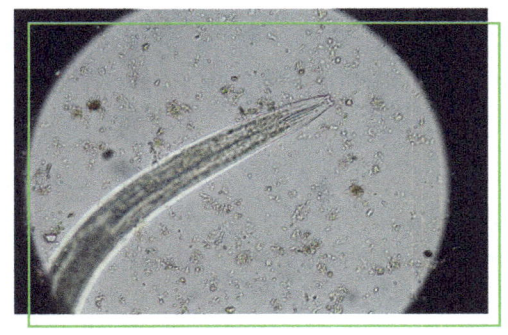

Nematodes are microscopic roundworms that inhabit the soil and play a multifaceted role in the soil food web. Nematodes can be both beneficial and harmful. Some nematodes are predators, actively seeking out and consuming other microscopic organisms like bacteria, fungi, and even other nematodes. These predatory nematodes act as natural pest controllers, helping manage harmful microorganisms that can damage plant roots and soil health. They contribute to maintaining a balanced and diverse soil ecosystem and can significantly impact soil health and plant growth.

However, not all nematodes are beneficial in the garden. Some are plant feeders, capable of damaging plant roots, leading to stunted growth and deficiencies. These plant-parasitic nematodes pose a challenge for gardeners as they can be very difficult to eliminate.

Nematodes also play a role in nutrient cycling and decomposition processes, similar to the other microbes we discussed earlier. When nematodes feed on microorganisms or organic matter, they release essential nutrients back into the soil, which your cannabis plants can then absorb.

MICROBIAL INOCULANTS

Understanding the roles of soil microbes allows us to utilize them for their benefits. Microbial inoculants are beneficial microorganisms applied either to the soil or the plant to enhance productivity and plant health. Using microbial inoculants offers numerous advantages, including enhanced nutrient uptake, disease suppression, improved soil structure, and reduced chemical usage.

- **Enhanced Nutrient Uptake:** As mentioned earlier, microbes break down organic matter, converting it into elements readily absorbed by plants.

- **Disease Suppression:** Some microbial inoculants protect plants from soil pathogens by competing with or inhibiting harmful microbes.

- **Improved Soil Structure:** Microbial inoculants contribute to soil aggregation, enhancing water retention and aeration.

- **Reduced Chemical Usage:** By promoting nutrient availability and disease resistance, microbial inoculants can reduce the need for synthetic fertilizers and pesticides.

Numerous microbial inoculant products are available on the market today, each with its own consortium of microbes. Some products I have personally used and recommend include Mammoth P, TeraGanix EM-1, DYNOMYCO, and Great White Mycorrhizae. It's important to note that you don't need to purchase and apply all these microbial inoculants. In fact, some gardeners rely solely on compost and/or worm castings, which already contain beneficial microorganisms. These microbial inoculant products provide an alternative method for introducing beneficial microbes to your soil.

HOW TO USE MICROBIAL INOCULANTS

When you look at the back of your microbial inoculant bottle or container, you'll see the ingredients and you'll also see the application rate. Not all microbial inoculants are created equal and the application rate mentioned should be followed. However, microbial inoculants are unlikely to cause harm if you slightly over or under apply them. Therefore, many gardeners will deviate from the manufacturers application rates as they see fit to meet the needs of their soil and plants. There are also a handful of general guidelines that you can follow in order to get the most out of them:

- **Choose Wisely:** Select inoculants that match your soil and plant needs. If you're looking to increase the bacterial population, choose a microbial inoculant that is mostly made up of bacteria species. If you're looking to increase the population of fungi, a mycorrhizal inoculant is a more appropriate choice.

- **Apply Correctly:** Follow the manufacturer's recommendations for applying inoculants as either a soil drench or foliar spray. Apply the dosage listed on the label at the specified frequency.

- **Timing Matters:** Use inoculants during the right stage of growth. For example, mycorrhizal inoculation is most effective during transplanting or early growth stages.

- **Monitor and Adjust:** Regularly assess plant health and soil condition to gauge the effectiveness of microbial inoculants. Adjust your inoculation strategy as needed to optimize results.

The soil food web is arguably the most important component supporting plant growth and soil health. Understanding the role of various microbes and utilizing microbial inoculants allows us to enhance the ecosystem in the soil and can result in better cannabis plant growth. By utilizing these microorganisms, we can reduce our reliance on synthetic fertilizers, promote healthier and more resilient plants, and ultimately cultivate a more environmentally responsible future for cannabis cultivation.

CHAPTER 11: PEST PREVENTION

PEST *Prevention*

One of the more frustrating aspects of organic gardening is battling pests. There are several pests out there that can wreak havoc on your plants, leaving you with stunted growth, deformed leaves, and often a disappointing harvest. Pest prevention is vital for the health and vitality of your plants. In this chapter, we'll dig into the importance of pest prevention, explore the top five most common garden pests, their signs of infection, and organic treatment methods. We will also discuss the principles of integrated pest management (IPM) as a sustainable approach to pest prevention.

THE IMPORTANCE OF PEST PREVENTION

Pest prevention is a key to successful gardening. There is nothing worse than seeing pests all over your cannabis plants and knowing you've done nothing to prevent them. If you ignore taking steps to prevent pests, it can lead to several downsides, including:

- **Plant Damage:** Garden pests can destroy your plants, reducing your yield and the quality of your harvest. This can be especially disheartening if you've invested a lot time and effort in maintaining your garden.

- **Spread of Disease:** Pests can carry and transmit diseases that can quickly infect your entire garden. This not only harms your current plants but can also impact future crops.

- **Increased Costs:** Treating a pest infestation after it has taken hold can be costly, both in terms of time and money. Preventing pests is often more efficient and economical than trying to eradicate them.

- **Frustration and Stress:** Dealing with a pest infestation can be emotionally taxing. Prevention reduces the stress and frustration associated with trying to save your garden from pests.

Understanding the adverse consequences of neglecting pest prevention should hopefully inspire you to invest the time in learning about some of the pests you might encounter and discover effective ways to prevent them from easily invading your garden.

TOP 5 COMMON GARDEN PESTS

When growing cannabis, you are more likely to encounter certain pests over others. If you do come across pests, knowing which pest it is and how to get rid of them will make things much easier for you. This section focuses on the top five most common garden pests, how to identify them, and organic treatment methods to eliminate them:

Fungus Gnats:

- **Signs of Infection:** Small, dark flies hovering around plants. Larvae are tiny, translucent worms in the soil.

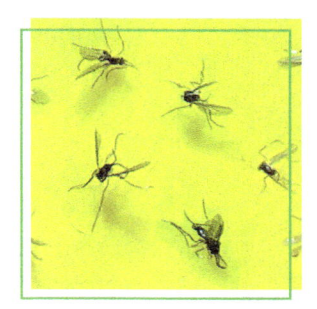

- **Organic Treatment:** Use yellow sticky traps to catch adult gnats. Allow the soil to dry between waterings to disrupt the larvae's life cycle. Apply beneficial nematodes to the soil to control larvae. Additionally, a fan blowing air over the soil will make it difficult for the adult fungus gnats to fly around and help dry the topsoil, making it inhospitable for them.

Spider Mites:

- **Signs of Infection:** Fine webbing, stippled leaves, and tiny, speck-like mites on the underside of leaves.

- **Organic Treatment:** Spray affected plants with a strong jet of water to dislodge mites. Apply neem oil or insecticidal soap to suffocate and repel them. Introduce cannabis-friendly predators that prey on spider mites, such as lacewings, big-eyed bugs, and ladybugs.

Aphids:

- **Signs of Infection:** Clusters of tiny, soft-bodied insects on plant stems and leaves. Sticky honeydew residue on leaves.

- **Organic Treatment:** Release ladybugs, lacewings, or parasitic wasps to feed on aphids. Spray plants with a mixture of water and dish soap to deter them. Other sprays that can be used include neem oil, cinnamon oil, eucalyptus oil, peppermint oil, cotton-seed oil, and coriander oil.

Thrips:

- **Signs of Infection:** Silvering or bronzing of leaves, distorted growth, and tiny, slender insects with fringed wings.

- **Organic Treatment:** Use yellow sticky traps to catch thrips. Spray with insecticidal soap. Introduce predatory mites like Orius insidiosus. Reflective mulches can deter thrips. Regularly remove and discard infested leaves.

Russet Mites:

- **Signs of Infection:** Yellowing, curling, and stunted growth of leaves. The presence of russet-colored mites under a magnifying glass.

- **Organic Treatment:** Prune and destroy infected plant parts. Apply organic miticides like neem oil or diatomaceous earth. Introduce natural predators such as Neoseiulus californicus, Galendromus occidentalis, and Amblyseius andersoni.

There are also various home remedies that you may encounter on the internet - some effective and some not effective at all. Additionally, a wide variety of products are available for sale that can eliminate various pests. Some products I have personally used and recommend include Mammoth CannControl and The Amazing Doctor Zymes. I like to use those products as a preventative measure or when I have an infestation, and both have worked extremely well for me. Other notable organic products include Essentria IC3, Azamax, and Spinosad.

With this information, you should now be able to identify common pests and apply organic treatment methods to reduce and eliminate their populations. Keep in mind that some pests, such as fungus gnats, are much easier to eradicate compared to others, like russet mites. Implementing pest prevention practices (which we will cover next) will significantly increase your chances of avoiding these pests altogether.

INTEGRATED PEST MANAGEMENT (IPM)

Integrated Pest Management (IPM) is a process that combines tools and strategies for managing and preventing pest infestations. There are various ways to prevent pests, and some methods are more effective than others. While we won't cover every single aspect of pest prevention in this book, we will discuss several general guidelines and approaches to help prevent pests from invading your garden and harming your plants. Here are some simple IPM methods you can implement today to ensure pests won't infest your garden:

- **Monitoring:** Make it a routine to inspect your plants regularly. Check both the upper and lower sides of leaves, stems, and soil for signs of pests. Personally, I inspect my plants daily, looking for things such as discoloration, wilting, chewed leaves, and the presence of insects and their eggs.

- **Cultural Practices:** Utilize companion plants to help deter or confuse pests. For instance, plants like garlic, chives, catnip, dill, and cilantro can repel aphids. Refer to the chapter on Companion Planting for more examples. Rotate crops in different areas of your garden each season to disrupt the life cycles of pests that target specific plants. Avoid overcrowding plants, as this can limit airflow and increase humidity, creating conditions conducive to pest infestations. Adding a mulch layer can create a barrier that makes it more challenging for pests to access the soil beneath it.

- **Biological Control:** Introduce beneficial insects, such as ladybugs, praying mantises, and parasitic wasps, to naturally control pest populations. Use beneficial nematodes in the soil to target soil-dwelling pests like root-feeding nematodes and fungus gnat larvae.

Mechanical Control: Use physical barriers like row covers, netting, or mesh to protect plants from flying insects, such as moths and butterflies. Regularly inspect your plants and manually remove pests when you spot them. This is effective for larger pests like caterpillars and slugs.

Pesticides: Some gardeners may choose to spray organic pesticides to prevent pests, while others use organic pesticides as a last resort. When using pesticides, opt for organic ones with minimal environmental impact and that are safe for beneficial insects. A general rule is to avoid spraying your plants when they are flowering, as some organic pesticides may stay on your buds, and the effects of consuming those buds afterward are not well known.

In summary, preventing pests from infiltrating your garden is essential for maintaining a healthy garden. Integrated Pest Management practices offer a sustainable, environmentally-friendly approach to keeping your garden pest-free while minimizing harm to beneficial organisms. By recognizing common pests, their signs of infection, and implementing organic treatment methods, you can act quickly to protect your plants and your harvest.

CHAPTER 12: COMPOST TEAS

COMPOST *Teas*

There are various optional methods that you can do when growing cannabis organically, brewing a compost tea is one of those methods. If created and applied correctly, compost teas can improve soil life, soil structure, and boost the health of your plants. In this chapter, we will cover what compost teas are, their benefits, types of compost teas, how to brew them, and how to apply them effectively to maximize their potential.

WHAT ARE COMPOST TEAS?

Compost teas are liquid solutions created by steeping compost or other organic materials in water. This process allows beneficial microorganisms, nutrients, and organic matter to be extracted into the water, resulting in a nutrient-rich, microbe-packed brew that can be applied directly to plants and soil. Compost teas come in various forms, including aerated compost teas, non-aerated compost teas, manure teas, and nutrient teas, each with its unique composition and purpose.

BENEFITS OF COMPOST TEAS

Compost teas offer a significant number of benefits for your garden. Here is a quick list of the benefits you can receive by creating and applying compost teas to your soil:

- **Improved Soil Health:** Compost teas improve soil structure, making it more conducive to nutrient absorption. They contribute to establishing a balanced ecosystem in your soil by introducing beneficial microorganisms.

- **Increased Nutrient Availability:** These teas release nutrients locked in organic matter, making them more accessible to plants. Essentially, the soluble nutrients become bioavailable, allowing plants to absorb them immediately.

- **Disease Suppression:** Beneficial microorganisms present in compost teas can help suppress harmful pathogens, reducing the risk of plant diseases.

- **Increased Plant Growth:** The added nutrients and beneficial microorganisms can lead to healthier, more vigorous plant growth, resulting in higher yields.

- **Environmental Benefits:** Compost teas recycle organic waste, reducing the need for you to purchase fertilizer.

Now that you know what compost teas are and their benefits, let's go over some of the different types of compost teas.

TYPES OF COMPOST TEAS

Compost teas come in various types, each serving distinct purposes. Some are designed primarily to boost microbial populations, while others focus on enhancing nutrient availability. Knowing the different categories of compost teas will assist you in choosing the most suitable one for your needs. It's worth noting that there are additional types of teas available beyond those discussed in this book. Below, we'll explore the three most common types used in cannabis cultivation.

- **Aerated Compost Tea (ACT):** This is the most common type of compost tea. It involves combining water, compost or worm castings, and a food source (such as molasses) within a container and then introducing oxygen using an air pump. This oxygenation promotes the multiplication of aerobic microorganisms present in the compost.

- **Non-Aerated Compost Tea:** Non-aerated compost tea offers simplicity as it requires fewer equipment and is easier to make. This method simply entails steeping compost in water. While non-aerated compost teas may lack the high microbial diversity of aerated versions, they still provide valuable nutrients and microorganisms.

- **Nutrient Tea:** Nutrient teas are customized blends mostly designed to address specific nutrient deficiencies in your soil. They are created by dissolving organic nutrient sources such as kelp meal, bone meal, or fish emulsion in water. Countless nutrient tea recipes can be found on the internet, allowing you to tailor them to your plant's growth stage, whether it's vegetative or flowering.

Since you now know the most common types of compost teas used in cannabis cultivation and what they are used for, let's get into the steps to brew compost teas.

BREWING COMPOST TEAS

Brewing compost teas may seem complex, but it's actually quite straightforward once you give it a try. Below, you'll find a step-by-step guide on how to make compost teas:

Equipment You'll Need:

- A large container or bucket
- Compost, worm castings, and/or nutrient blend
- Dechlorinated water
- Unsulfured molasses
- Air pump (not needed for non-aerated compost tea)
- Air stones (not needed for non-aerated compost tea)

Steps:

1. Fill the container or bucket with dechlorinated water. I typically use a 5-gallon bucket and fill it with 4 gallons of water, leaving some space at the top to prevent spills when the air pump is on.

2. Place approximately 1-2 cups of compost, worm castings, or your nutrient blend for every 4 gallons of water inside a mesh bag or directly into the bucket.

3. Add 1 tablespoon of unsulfured blackstrap molasses per gallon of water as a microbial food source. Warming the molasses before adding it to your bucket will help it mix better.

4. Set up the aeration system, ensuring that air stones are evenly spaced and submerged in the water. Allow it to aerate for 24 hours. If you're creating non-aerated compost tea, simply stir the solution 2-3 times within 24 hours.

5. After brewing, strain the compost tea to remove solids. Apply it immediately to your garden.

The steps mentioned above represent just one way to brew compost teas. There are various ways to customize the process by adjusting the amount of water, compost or worm castings, nutrient blends, the type and amount of food source, brewing duration, dilution ratio, and more. This serves as a basic overview of the brewing process, and feel free to make modifications that best suit your garden's needs.

WHEN AND HOW TO APPLY COMPOST TEAS

The timing and application rate of compost teas depend on your garden's specific needs. For instance, if your plants are showing signs of one or more nutrient deficiencies, you might want to brew a nutrient tea to enhance soil nutrition. Conversely, if you've recently applied organic amendments and wish to increase the microbial population for decomposition, brewing an aerated compost tea with compost or worm castings can be beneficial. Start by considering the desired outcome of the tea and then work backward to determine the appropriate type, inputs, and brewing method.

As for frequency, that also varies according to your garden's specific requirements. If your goal is to boost the soil's microbial population, it's generally recommended to brew and apply compost tea every two weeks. However, some gardeners choose to use compost teas less frequently, such as once a month.

Most batches of compost tea can be used at full strength without adverse effects. However, many gardeners prefer to dilute the tea with dechlorinated water to create a less potent solution. The general guideline is to dilute the tea to a ratio of at least 1:4 (4 cups of compost tea to 1 gallon of water), and some individuals dilute it further, at a ratio of 1:10.

Compost teas can also serve as an effective foliar spray to help prevent disease outbreaks. When using them for foliar applications, dilute the tea with water at a 1:10 ratio. Apply it early in the morning or late in the evening to avoid damaging foliage in direct sunlight.

It's important to note that compost teas are optional. You can successfully complete a growing cycle without using them. While some gardeners create compost teas every cycle and consider them essential, you can view them as a valuable tool in your gardening toolkit, to be used only when truly necessary.

CHAPTER 13: COVER CROPS

COVER *Crops*

Cover crops are specific plant species cultivated primarily to protect and enrich the soil. Unlike cash crops grown for harvest, cover crops are cultivated for their ecological benefits rather than their economic value. They can be grown either during the cannabis grow cycle alongside your plants or independently between grow cycles. Cover crops play a pivotal role in sustainable agriculture by preventing soil erosion, suppressing weeds, enhancing soil structure, improving nutrient cycling, and fostering biodiversity.

BENEFITS OF COVER CROPS

Using cover crops in your garden is optional; you can successfully complete the grow cycle without them. However, many gardeners highly recommend using them due to the numerous benefits they offer:

- **Erosion Control:** Cover crops act as a natural shield, protecting the soil from erosion caused by wind and water. Their extensive root systems anchor the soil, preventing it from washing or blowing away during heavy rains or strong winds.

- **Weed Suppression:** Cover crops compete with weeds for sunlight, water, and nutrients. This competition significantly reduces weed populations, thus decreasing the need for herbicides and manual weed control.

- **Soil Health Improvement:** Cover crops enhance soil fertility and structure. They capture and store nutrients like nitrogen and phosphorus, preventing leaching into groundwater. When these cover crops decompose, they release these stored nutrients back into the soil, making them available for your cannabis plants to absorb.

- **Biodiversity Promotion:** Different cover crop species attract various beneficial insects, increasing biodiversity in your garden. This can effectively help control pests and enhance pollination for other crops.

- **Disease and Pest Suppression:** Some cover crops release natural compounds that inhibit the growth of certain pathogens and pests, reducing the need for pesticide applications.

TYPES OF COVER CROPS

There are various types of cover crops, each with unique characteristics and benefits. In this section, we will explore three major categories:

Broadleaves:

Broadleaf cover crops are characterized by their wide, flat leaves and diverse species. Some common examples include:

- **Buckwheat:** A quick-growing cover crop that excels at suppressing weeds. It also has a fibrous root system that penetrates the soil, improving its structure and porosity.

- **Mustard:** Known for its biofumigation properties, mustard can suppress nematodes and soilborne pathogens while contributing to organic matter.

- **Alyssum:** Alyssum attracts beneficial insects like hoverflies and parasitic wasps, aiding in pest control.

Legumes:

Leguminous cover crops are nitrogen-fixing plants that form symbiotic relationships with nitrogen-fixing bacteria. They include:

- **Peas:** Peas enrich the soil with nitrogen through their root nodules, improving soil fertility.

- **Soybeans:** Soybeans are excellent nitrogen fixers and provide additional organic matter to the soil upon decomposition.

- **Clover:** Clover fixes nitrogen and reduces soil erosion.

- **Vetch:** Vetch is a hardy cover crop that fixes nitrogen and is known for its resilience in various soil types.

Grains:

Grain cover crops consist of annual grasses and are chosen for their ability to suppress weeds, improve soil structure, and scavenge nutrients. Notable examples include:

- **Rye:** Rye has an extensive root system that improves soil structure. It is an effective weed suppressor and is winter-hardy.

- **Oats:** Oats are fast-growing and provide excellent erosion control. They also scavenge excess nutrients from the soil.

- **Wheat:** Wheat can be sown as a cover crop, providing ground cover and contributing organic matter when incorporated.

It's also worth considering cover crop mixtures. For example, there are 'cover crop blends' available online that include 12 or more species of cover crops. Combining different species of cover crops can provide numerous benefits for both the plants and the soil. Now that you are familiar with the three major categories of cover crops and some of the plants that fall within them, let's continue onto when and how to grow them and determine the appropriate quantities.

TIMING AND APPLICATION RATES

The success of cover crops largely depends on proper timing and application rates. Factors such as climate, soil type, and the desired impact on soil health should all be considered when selecting the most suitable cover crop for cannabis cultivation.

Broadleaves are better suited to grow alongside cannabis during its active growth cycle. Their rapid growth and dense foliage provide effective weed suppression and prevent competition with the cannabis plants. Legumes are also beneficial when cultivated simultaneously with cannabis, as they enrich the soil with nitrogen, supporting cannabis' nutrient needs. On the other hand, grains are ideal for planting between cannabis grow cycles.

These grains can protect the soil from erosion, scavenge excess nutrients, and improve soil structure, all while not interfering with the cannabis plants' growth when they are actively growing.

The number of seeds to plant for an effective cover crop depends on several factors, including the specific cover crop species, the size of the area to be covered, and the desired planting density. When growing indoors in containers, a general guideline is to sow the seeds with a spacing of around 1-2 inches apart in rows. Outdoor cover crop seeding rates can vary widely, ranging from 15 to 50 pounds of seed per acre. It's crucial to note that different cover crop species may have specific seeding rate recommendations, so consulting the rates provided on the seed package is essential since they can vary significantly.

For small home growers, simply spreading the seeds by hand can suffice without the need for additional equipment. However, if you are growing outdoors on a larger scale or in a farming setting, you can utilize seeding equipment such as broadcast seeders, grain drills, or no-till drills. The choice of equipment depends on your specific farming system and the type of cover crop you are planting. These tools ensure even distribution and proper soil contact, which are crucial for successful planting.

CHAPTER 14: MULCH LAYERS

MULCH *Layers*

Mulch layers play a vital role in maintaining the health and productivity of your garden. A mulch layer is a protective covering spread over the soil's surface, designed to conserve moisture, suppress weeds, regulate temperature, and more. A well-mulched garden not only looks attractive but also offers a range of benefits. In this chapter, we will explore the world of mulch layers, focusing on their various types, benefits, and the top organic mulches commonly used by cannabis gardeners. We will also discuss application methods and rates to ensure you get the most out of your mulch.

BENEFITS OF MULCH LAYERS

Mulch layers, while an optional method, offer several advantages for your garden:

- **Moisture Conservation:** Mulch acts as a barrier, reducing soil evaporation, helping maintain consistent moisture levels, and reducing the need for frequent watering.

- **Weed Suppression:** A layer of mulch prevents sunlight from reaching the soil, preventing weed germination and competition with your cannabis plants.

- **Temperature Regulation:** Mulch helps regulate soil temperature, keeping it cooler in hot weather and warmer in cold weather, creating a stable environment for your plants' root systems and microbial populations.

- **Erosion Control:** Mulch reduces the impact of heavy rain and prevents soil erosion, protecting your garden from damage.

- **Improved Soil Structure:** Organic mulches break down over time, enriching the soil with organic matter and nutrients, enhancing soil structure and fertility.

ORGANIC VS. INORGANIC MULCHES

Organic mulches are crafted from natural materials that decompose over time, enriching the soil as they break down and providing numerous benefits for your garden. In contrast, inorganic mulches, like gravel, plastic, and rubber, do not decompose and are typically reserved for specific purposes such as weed control and aesthetics. These inorganic options are less commonly used in cannabis cultivation; therefore, this chapter will focus on organic mulches for cannabis cultivation.

TOP 5 ORGANIC MULCHES

Now that we've discussed the benefits of mulch and the differences between organic and inorganic options, let's focus on the top five organic mulches commonly used in cannabis gardens:

Wood Chips: Made from shredded tree branches and bark, wood chips are widely used in cannabis gardens. They break down slowly, providing long-term benefits.

- **When to Use:** Throughout the grow cycle.

- **How to Apply:** Spread a 2 to 4-inch layer around your plants, avoiding direct contact with stems.

Straw: Straw is an excellent mulch for cannabis gardens. It's lightweight and easy to work with. As it decomposes, it adds nutrients to the soil.

- **When to Use:** Throughout the grow cycle.

- **How to Apply:** Lay a 2 to 4-inch layer between rows or around plants, ensuring good coverage.

Compost: Compost can also be used as mulch. It's rich in nutrients and improves soil structure. Ensure it has undergone sufficient decomposition before applying it to ensure nutrient availability.

- **When to Use:** Throughout the grow cycle; keep in mind that you may need to apply less fertilizer since compost is nutrient-rich.

- **How to Apply:** Spread a 1 to 2-inch layer around plants, avoiding direct contact with stems.

Leaves: Shredded leaves are a fantastic and cost-effective mulch. As leaves fall off your plants or you defoliate, drop them onto the soil. They decompose relatively quickly and add organic matter to the soil.

- **When to Use:** Throughout the grow cycle.

- **How to Apply:** Spread a 2 to 4-inch layer over the soil surface.

Grass Clippings: Grass clippings make an excellent mulch if they are free from herbicides and pesticides. They break down quickly and add nitrogen to the soil.

- **When to Use:** Use grass clippings cautiously throughout the grow cycle, as they quickly break down and can lead to over-fertilization if used too often.

- **How to Apply:** Spread a thin 1/2 to 1-inch layer around plants, avoiding thick mats.

The above information on when to use mulch layers and their application rates provides general guidelines. Some growers may deviate from these recommendations and still obtain excellent results. Regardless of the method you use to apply organic mulch layers, remember that they will decompose over time, so it's important to monitor and regularly replenish them to maintain their benefits. Armed with this knowledge, you can make informed decisions on how to use mulch to enhance both plant growth and soil health.

CHAPTER 15: COMPANION PLANTING

COMPANION *Planting*

The concept of companion planting has been practiced for centuries, and for good reason. This age-old technique involves strategically planting different types of plants together to create a mutually beneficial environment. When it comes to cannabis cultivation, companion planting can be a game-changer. In this chapter, we'll dig into what companion planting is, explore its benefits, and discuss the top five companion plants to cultivate alongside cannabis. We'll also provide guidance on when and how to incorporate these companions into your cannabis garden.

WHAT IS COMPANION PLANTING?

Companion planting is a gardening strategy based on the idea that certain plants, when grown together, can support each other's growth and deter pests. This practice involves selecting plants that have complementary characteristics, such as their growth habits, root systems, and chemical defenses, to create a harmonious garden ecosystem.

The benefits of companion planting are multifaceted. Below is a quick list of the benefits you can obtain when utilizing companion planting in your cannabis garden:

- **Pest Control:** Certain companion plants can help deter or confuse common cannabis pests, reducing the need to use pesticides.

- **Improved Soil Health:** Companion plants can improve soil structure and fertility, making it more conducive to cannabis growth.

- **Biodiversity:** A diverse garden is more resilient and less susceptible to disease outbreaks.

- **Increased Yields:** By carefully selecting companion plants, you can create an environment that maximizes the potential of your cannabis plants.

Now that you understand the basics of companion planting, let's explore the top five companion plants for cannabis cultivation and how they can benefit your garden.

TOP 5 COMPANION PLANTS FOR CANNABIS

Marigolds

Marigolds are a popular choice for companion planting due to their ability to deter a wide range of common cannabis pests, including aphids and nematodes. Their strong aroma acts as a natural repellent, masking the scent of your cannabis plants. Additionally, marigolds enhance soil health by secreting allelopathic chemicals that suppress weed growth, leaving more nutrients and space for your cannabis.

Mint

Mint is a versatile herb that can thrive in various garden conditions. It's known for its strong fragrance, which helps mask the scent of cannabis and deter pests. Mint also has a remarkable ability to repel rodents, making it a valuable addition to outdoor cannabis gardens.

Basil

Basil is an aromatic herb that not only complements your cannabis garden with its culinary uses but also acts as a natural insect repellent. It's particularly effective against flies, mosquitoes, and aphids. The oils produced by basil plants can deter pests and is even said to enhance the flavor of your cannabis buds.

Nasturtium

Nasturtiums are not only visually appealing with their bright orange and yellow flowers but also serve as a sacrificial crop. They attract aphids and caterpillars away from your cannabis plants, essentially acting as a trap crop. Nasturtiums also release compounds into the soil that deter certain pests and improve soil health.

Chamomile

Chamomile is a soothing and aromatic herb that makes an excellent companion plant for cannabis. It has numerous benefits for your garden, including its ability to deter common pests like aphids and beetles. Chamomile's delicate, daisy-like flowers also attract beneficial insects such as hoverflies and parasitic wasps, which can help keep harmful pests at bay. Also, chamomile is known for its calming and anti-fungal properties, making it a valuable addition to your garden's ecosystem.

As you've just learned, certain companion plants offer multiple advantages, and the range of potential companions extends beyond what we've covered here. There is a diverse selection of other plants that you can integrate into your cannabis garden, each with its unique benefits. As you progress on your path to organic cannabis cultivation, I urge you to explore additional resources to discover more varieties of companion plants that can be effectively incorporated into your garden.

INCORPORATING COMPANION PLANTS INTO YOUR GARDEN

To optimize the benefits of companion planting in your garden, follow these guidelines:

- **Plan Your Layout:** Design your garden layout to maximize the advantages of companion planting. Consider the growth habits and spacing requirements of both cannabis and companion plants.

- **Companion Plant Selection:** Choose companion plants that are compatible with your growing environment. Research each companion plant's specific benefits and care requirements.

- **Plant Placement:** Strategically place companion plants throughout your cannabis garden. For example, position marigolds or nasturtiums along the perimeter to create a protective barrier.

- **Maintenance:** Routinely monitor your companion plants for signs of pests or disease. Address any issues promptly to prevent them from spreading to your cannabis.

- **Crop Rotation:** Implement crop rotation to help prevent pests and diseases. Change the location of your cannabis and companion plants each growing season.

- **Harvest and Enjoy:** Many companion plants, such as basil and lavender, offer culinary or medicinal uses. Harvest and enjoy them to reap these additional benefits.

Incorporating companion plants into your cannabis garden can promote a healthier and more productive growing environment. By thoughtfully selecting and caring for your companion plants, you'll not only enhance your cannabis but you'll also establish a balanced and diverse garden ecosystem.

CHAPTER 16: EARTHWORMS

EARTHWORMS

Earthworms, often referred to as just 'worms,' are among the most underrated organisms in the garden. While technically not essential for completing a cannabis grow cycle, they play a crucial role in maintaining soil health and promoting plant growth in organic gardens. In this chapter, we will uncover the world of earthworms, exploring their different types and the benefits they bring to your garden. We'll also discuss when and how to introduce them to your garden to maximize their positive impact.

WHAT ARE EARTHWORMS?

Earthworms are soft-bodied, segmented worms that reside in soil. They play a critical role in maintaining soil health by enhancing aeration, recycling nutrients, and improving soil structure. Typically, they are brownish or reddish-brown in color and can vary in size, ranging from a few inches to several inches, depending on the species. Earthworms have silently worked beneath the soil's surface for millions of years, performing essential functions that directly benefit plant growth.

BENEFITS OF EARTHWORMS IN THE GARDEN

There are numerous benefits to be gained in your garden through the utilization of earthworms.

- **Soil Aeration:** Earthworm movement within the soil creates channels, facilitating the penetration of air and water deep into the ground. This boosts soil aeration, enabling plant roots to access essential oxygen, nutrients, and water.

- **Nutrient Recycling:** Earthworms consume organic matter like compost and decaying leaves, transforming it into nutrient-rich castings. These castings are rich in vital nutrients such as nitrogen, phosphorus, and potassium, serving as an excellent natural fertilizer for your garden.

- **Improved Soil Structure:** Earthworms' continuous burrowing and feeding activities enhance soil structure, resulting in a crumbly texture that retains moisture effectively. This improved structure also minimizes compaction, ensuring ample space for plant roots to grow.

- **Enhanced Microbial Activity:** Earthworms stimulate beneficial microbial activity in the soil. Through their digestion of organic matter, they release enzymes and create a microenvironment that promotes the growth of beneficial bacteria and fungi. These microorganisms further contribute to nutrient breakdown and availability.

TYPES OF EARTHWORMS

There are three main types of earthworms that cannabis gardeners typically add to their gardens:

RED WIGGLERS

Red wigglers, also known as red composting worms, are small and slender earthworms, typically measuring 2 to 4 inches in length. They have a reddish-brown color and thrive in compost piles and bins. While they are well-known for decomposing kitchen waste into nutrient-rich compost, they also perform great in garden beds.

EUROPEAN NIGHTCRAWLERS

European nightcrawlers are larger than red wigglers, measuring 3 to 6 inches in length. They are light pinkish-gray in color and can be found in compost bins and garden beds. These earthworms are noted for their ability to burrow deeper into the soil, enhancing soil aeration and nutrient distribution.

AFRICAN NIGHTCRAWLERS

African nightcrawlers are among the largest earthworms, often reaching lengths of 6 to 8 inches. They are reddish-brown to purplish-gray in color and are known for their capacity to burrow deep into the soil, even deeper than the European nightcrawlers we just covered. These earthworms thrive in warm, moist conditions, making them excellent choices for gardeners in tropical and subtropical climates. While they excel in composting, many gardeners also add them to their large containers of soil, where they effectively aerate the bottom layer.

WHEN & HOW TO ADD EARTHWORMS

The decision of when and how many earthworms to introduce into your garden depends on several factors, including the type of worm and the size of your garden. Here are some guidelines:

- **Timing:** If you are growing cannabis outdoors, the best time to introduce earthworms to your garden is during the spring or fall when the soil is moderately moist, and temperatures are milder. Earthworms are most active during these seasons, making it easier for them to establish themselves. If you are growing cannabis indoors, earthworms can be introduced at any point in the grow cycle.

- **Soil Preparation:** Before adding earthworms, ensure that your garden soil is well-prepared. Remove any debris, rocks, or compacted soil, and amend it with organic matter such as compost, organic fertilizer blend, or aged manure to create an inviting environment for the worms.

- **Distribution:** To distribute the earthworms evenly, dig shallow holes or trenches throughout your garden bed and place the worms in them. Cover the earthworms with soil, lightly water the soil, and provide a layer of mulch to retain moisture and regulate temperature.

- **Monitor and Maintain:** Regularly monitor your garden's soil moisture and adjust watering as needed to keep it consistently moist, but not waterlogged. As the earthworm population grows, they will continue to improve your soil's health and fertility.

The number of red wigglers, European nightcrawlers, or African nightcrawlers you should add to your garden depends on several factors, including the size of the container or bed and whether or not worms are already present in the soil. Here are some general guidelines:

- **Red Wigglers:** You can start with approximately 500 to 1000 red wigglers for a 10-gallon container or 1 to 2 square feet of space in an outdoor area. If worms are already in the soil, adding around 200 to 400 may be sufficient for soil improvement.

- **European Nightcrawlers:** You can start with about 200 to 400 European nightcrawlers for a 10-gallon container or 2 to 4 square feet of space in an outdoor area. Similar to red wigglers, if worms are already in the soil, a smaller number, around 100 to 200, may be adequate.

- **African Nightcrawlers:** You can start with around 100 to 200 African nightcrawlers in a 10-gallon container or 1 to 2 square feet in an outdoor area. If worms are already in the soil, adding an additional 50 to 100 African nightcrawlers should be sufficient.

In summary, while earthworms aren't a required addition to your organic garden, they can greatly enhance it. By understanding the types of earthworms available, when to add them, and how to add them, you can utilize their incredible benefits to increase soil and plant health.

CHAPTER 17: BENEFICIAL INSECTS

BENEFICIAL *Insects*

*H*earing the term "beneficial insects" may sound like a contradiction, but these organisms play a vital role in maintaining a healthy, pest-free garden. In this chapter, we will explore what beneficial insects are, their advantages, and the most common ones suitable for your cannabis garden. We will also discuss the timing, methods, and quantities for introducing them to your garden.

WHAT ARE BENEFICIAL INSECTS?

An insect is a small invertebrate animal with 6 legs. When we talk about 'beneficial insects' we are talking about a diverse group of insects that aids in controlling garden pests and enhancing the overall health of your plants. In contrast to harmful pests, these insects are your allies, offering several benefits to your garden. Here is a list of advantages you can gain when beneficial insects are present:

- **Natural Pest Control:** Beneficial insects prey on harmful pests like aphids, caterpillars, and mites, reducing the need for pesticide applications.

- **Pollination:** Many beneficial insects, such as bees and butterflies, are excellent pollinators. Although they are not required for cannabis plant pollination, they contribute to the reproduction of other flowering plants, like fruits and vegetables, leading to increased production.

- **Biodiversity:** Encouraging a diverse insect population promotes a balanced ecosystem in your garden.

COMMON BENEFICIAL INSECTS

While numerous beneficial insects exist, a select few are particularly effective in supporting cannabis gardens. Here are six beneficial insects and how they are helpful to your garden:

1. **Ladybugs:** These voracious predators consume aphids, mealybugs, leafhoppers, and insect eggs.

2. **Lacewings:** Lacewings feed on aphids, mites, and small caterpillars.

3. **Praying Mantises:** Praying mantises are versatile predators, targeting flies, moths, and grasshoppers.

4. **Springtails:** Springtails aid in the breakdown and decomposition of organic matter, while their movement through the soil contributes to aeration and helps prevent soil compaction.

5. **Rove Beetles:** Ground-dwelling rove beetles help control soil pests, particularly those in mulch and organic matter. Some species also feed on mites, beetle larvae, aphids, and small caterpillars, both as adults and larvae.

6. **Predator Mites:** While not classified as insects due to their eight legs (in contrast to insects with six legs), predator mites play a similar role in pest control. They consume the eggs, nymphs, and adults of various spider mites, along with other plant-feeding mites like rust mites and bulb mites.

WHEN & HOW TO ADD BENEFICIAL INSECTS

Depending on the beneficial insect, there are several methods for introducing them to your garden. Many can be released simply by opening the container they come in and allowing them to fly or crawl out. Ensure the area is well-watered so they can find immediate food and shelter. Timing is important when introducing beneficial insects to your garden; release them when the target pests are active and in vulnerable stages of their life cycle. Early morning or late evening is often the best time for release, as insects are less active and more likely to remain in the area.

The quantity of beneficial insects you release should be based on the size of your garden and the severity of your pest problem. Generally, follow the recommendations provided on the packaging of the beneficial insects you purchase. Keep in mind that it's often more effective to release small quantities of insects at regular intervals rather than a single large release.

CHAPTER 18: COMPOSTING

COMPOSTING

*I*magine if you could use junk mail and leftover food to provide your plant with the nutrients needed for growth. You can actually achieve this through a process called composting! Composting is an organic recycling process where materials like leaves and kitchen scraps are transformed into a fertilizer that you can add to your soil, providing your plants with the essential elements for growth. Composting accelerates the natural decomposition of organic matter by creating an optimal habitat for microorganisms, such as bacteria, fungi, and decomposers like worms, sowbugs, and nematodes. The result of this breakdown, which often resembles soil, is called compost. Compost is often referred to as 'black gold' due to its dark color and the massive benefits it provides to the soil. In this chapter, we will explore the benefits of composting, go over four different composting methods, and provide the process for each of them. We will also reveal how to determine when your compost is ready and the application rate for optimal results.

BENEFITS OF COMPOSTING

Before diving into the different composting methods, let's first understand why composting is such a valuable practice:

- **Enriches Soil:** Compost adds essential nutrients, such as nitrogen, phosphorus, and potassium, to your soil. It improves soil structure, making it easier for plants to access these nutrients and retain moisture.

- **Reduces Waste:** Composting diverts organic waste from landfills, reducing the production of harmful methane gas. It's an eco-friendly way to manage kitchen scraps, yard trimmings, and more.

- **Enhances Plant Health:** Compost contains beneficial microorganisms that suppress plant diseases and pests, creating a healthier environment for your plants.

- **Saves Money:** By creating your compost, you reduce the need for store-bought fertilizers, saving you money in the long run.

TYPES OF COMPOSTING

There are various composting methods. Let's go over the four most-common methods:

1. Open Air Composting

Open air composting is one of the most common and traditional methods of composting. It involves creating a compost pile and then allowing the organic materials added to decompose naturally through exposure to the elements. Here's the open air composting process in more detail:

Process:

1. **Location:** Choose a suitable location in your yard or garden for open air composting. It should have good drainage to prevent waterlogging and receive partial sunlight for optimal decomposition.

2. **Compost Bin or Area:** While it's possible to create an open compost pile directly on the ground, many people prefer to use a compost bin or designated area to contain the materials and keep the compost neat. Bins can be homemade or purchased, but they should allow for aeration.

3. **Layering:** Composting is all about balancing the "browns" and "greens." Browns include materials like dried leaves, paper, straw, and cardboard, while greens consist of kitchen scraps, grass clippings, and fresh yard waste. Layer these materials alternately in the compost pile or bin. Browns provide carbon, while greens offer nitrogen, and this balance is essential for the composting process.

4. **Aeration:** To facilitate decomposition, it's important to turn or mix the compost pile regularly. This introduces oxygen, which is crucial for the activity of aerobic microorganisms that break down the materials. Mixing every few weeks or when the temperature in the pile rises is a good practice.

5   **Moisture:** Maintaining the right moisture level is important. The compost pile should feel like a wrung-out sponge. If it's too dry, sprinkle some water; if it's too wet, add more dry materials (browns).

6   **Time:** Open air composting is a slow process. Depending on factors like temperature, pile size, and the materials used, it can take anywhere from 6 to 12 months or longer for the compost to be fully mature.

7   **Monitoring:** Keep an eye on your compost pile. Over time, it will begin to change in appearance, becoming dark, crumbly, and earthy-smelling. These are signs that your compost is ready to use.

2. Direct Composting

Direct composting, also known as trench composting, involves burying organic waste directly in the garden where it decomposes and becomes usable nutrients for your plants. Here's the process for direct composting:

Process:

1   **Site Selection:** Choose the area in your garden bed where you want to apply direct composting. Ensure that it's an appropriate location for planting and that it receives adequate sunlight and drainage.

2   **Trench or Hole:** Using a shovel, dig a trench or hole in your selected garden bed. The depth of the trench typically ranges from 12 to 18 inches, depending on the available space and your garden's specific requirements.

3   **Adding Organic Waste:** Place your kitchen scraps and other organic materials directly into the trench or hole. These can include fruit and vegetable peels, coffee grounds, eggshells, and garden debris. Avoid adding diseased plant materials or anything that could attract pests.

4. **Cover and Mix:** Cover the organic waste with soil, ensuring it is thoroughly mixed with the soil to encourage decomposition. You can also add a layer of shredded leaves or compost to help with the decomposition process.

5. **Planting:** You can plant your plants directly over the trench where you've buried the organic waste. Make sure to leave enough space between the plants and the composted area to avoid harming their roots.

6. **Maintenance:** Water your garden as you normally would, keeping in mind that the buried organic matter will gradually release nutrients into the soil as it decomposes. Monitor the growth of your plants and adjust your watering and feeding routine as needed.

3. Vermicomposting

Vermicomposting is a specialized and highly efficient form of composting that relies on the activities of earthworms to break down organic matter into nutrient-packed castings. These castings, also known as worm poop, are a valuable soil conditioner and fertilizer. Vermicomposting is an excellent method for those with limited space or who wish to compost indoors. Here's the vermicomposting process in more detail:

Process:

1. **Select a Bin:** Begin by choosing a suitable container or bin for your vermicomposting operation. This can be a commercially available worm bin or a DIY bin, but it should have proper drainage and ventilation to ensure a healthy environment for the worms.

2. **Bedding Material:** Prepare a bedding material for your worms. Shredded newspaper, cardboard, or coconut coir are excellent choices. Dampen the bedding material until it reaches the consistency of a wrung-out sponge.

3. **Add Worms:** Introduce worms to the bin. The most common type of worm for vermicomposting is Red Wigglers. These worms are voracious decomposers and thrive in the composting environment. Other types of worms that can be used are European Nightcrawlers and African Nightcrawlers. More information on these types of worms are in the Worms chapter.

4. **Feeding:** Begin adding kitchen scraps and other organic materials to the bin. Kitchen scraps can include fruit and vegetable peels, coffee grounds, eggshells, and similar organic waste. Avoid adding meat, dairy, and oily or acidic foods.

5. **Layering:** Alternate layers of kitchen scraps with the bedding material. This provides the worms with a balanced diet and helps control moisture levels. Keep the bin covered with a breathable lid to maintain the appropriate humidity.

6. **Maintenance:** Regularly check the moisture level of the bedding, ensuring that it remains damp but not waterlogged. Worms need moisture to breathe, so mist the bedding with water if it becomes too dry.

7. **Harvesting:** After several months, you can harvest the worm castings by gently removing the top layer of bedding and compost. Worm castings resemble dark, crumbly soil. You can use them directly in your garden to improve soil quality or create a nutrient-rich worm tea by steeping the castings in water and using it as a liquid fertilizer. More information on creating teas is in the Compost Teas chapter.

4. Bokashi Composting

Bokashi composting is a unique and odorless method of composting that employs anaerobic fermentation using a specialized bran inoculated with beneficial microbes. Unlike traditional composting methods, Bokashi composting can handle a wider range of organic materials, including cooked food and meat scraps. This method is ideal for those with limited space or those who prefer an indoor composting solution. Here's the process for Bokashi composting:

Process:

1. **Bokashi Bucket:** Start by obtaining a Bokashi composting bucket with a tight-sealing lid. These containers are airtight and typically come with a drainage system to collect excess liquid produced during the fermentation process.

2. **Bokashi Bran:** Purchase or make Bokashi bran, which is a mix of wheat bran or rice bran infused with beneficial microbes. It helps ferment the organic waste quickly and efficiently.

3. **Layering:** Add a layer of Bokashi bran to the bottom of your Bokashi bucket. This provides the initial inoculation of microbes. Then, begin adding your organic waste. Unlike traditional composting, you can include a wide range of materials, such as cooked food, dairy, meat, and even small bones.

4. **Compact and Press:** After each addition of organic waste, compact it down and press out any excess air. The goal is to create an anaerobic environment within the bucket.

5. **Seal Tightly:** Ensure that the Bokashi bucket is sealed tightly after each addition of waste. This prevents the entry of oxygen, which is essential for the fermentation process.

6 **Fermentation:** Store the sealed Bokashi bucket in a cool, dark place. Over the next two weeks, the waste will undergo fermentation. You may notice a slightly sour smell, which is normal.

7 **Drainage:** As the waste ferments, excess liquid may collect in the drainage system. This liquid, known as "Bokashi juice," is a nutrient-rich liquid fertilizer that you can dilute with water and use in your garden. A general dilution rate is a 1:100 ratio.

8 **Second Bucket:** Once the first Bokashi bucket is full and fermented, start filling a second bucket while the first one continues to ferment. The first bucket can sit for a few weeks to several months while the waste further breaks down.

9 **Finishing:** The fermented waste is not yet fully composted and will need further processing. You can either bury it in your garden or add it to a traditional compost pile to complete the decomposition process.

APPLICATION RATE

Your compost is ready to use when it is dark, crumbly, and has an earthy smell. Also, the inputs should be completely broken down. The ideal application rate can vary depending on what's in your soil and the stage of growth your plant is in. As a general guideline, spread a 1-2 inch layer of compost evenly over your garden beds. Gently work it into the top few inches of soil using a rake or your hands. Avoid smothering plant roots with compost and leave a few inches of space around stems.

CHAPTER 19: SOIL RECIPES

SOIL *Recipes*

While some gardeners are satisfied with their available soil, others choose to create a custom soil mix. They do this either to save money or to ensure that their cannabis plants have precisely the right nutrients in the ideal proportions. In this chapter, we will explore the benefits of creating your own custom soil mix. We will also provide detailed instructions for two popular soil mixtures: ClackamasCoot Soil Mix and Subcool's Super Soil.

CUSTOM SOIL BENEFITS

Creating a customized soil blend offers several advantages for gardeners, especially those cultivating a specialty crop like cannabis. Here are some reasons why following a soil recipe is beneficial:

- **Nutrient Control:** Soil recipes allow you to manage the nutrient content of your growing medium. Different plants have distinct nutrient requirements at different growth stages. By following a soil recipe, you can tailor the nutrient profile to meet your plants' specific needs, ensuring optimal growth and development.

- **Enhanced Aeration and Drainage:** Custom soil blends can enhance aeration and drainage, preventing issues like root rot and excessive moisture. Well-aerated soil promotes root health by supplying oxygen to the root zone and facilitating gas exchange between roots and soil.

- **Reduced Dependency on Fertilizers:** Incorporating organic matter such as compost and worm castings along with beneficial microorganisms creates a self-sustaining ecosystem that gradually provides nutrients to your plants. This reduces the need to purchase additional fertilizers.

- **Pest and Disease Resistance:** Some soil recipes include ingredients that deter pests and diseases. This natural resistance can decrease the likelihood of infestations and protect your plants without resorting to pesticide application.

Now that you understand the benefits of using a custom soil mix, let's dive into the specifics of two popular soil recipes:

CLACKAMASCOOT SOIL MIX

The ClackamasCoot Soil Mix is a popular organic soil mixture developed by a cannabis cultivation expert known as "ClackamasCoot." This soil mix is specifically designed for growing cannabis plants but can be used for other crops as well. The mix consists of a 1:1:1 ratio, which includes:

Ingredients:

- 1 part high-quality compost
- 1 part coconut coir or peat moss
- 1 part perlite

Additionally, it includes inputs to enhance soil structure and moisture retention, along with organic amendments to supply the necessary nutrition for your cannabis plants:

- 1/2 part vermiculite
- 1/2 part pumice
- 1/2 part earthworm castings
- 1/2 part basalt rock dust
- 1/2 part gypsum
- 1/2 part oyster shell flour
- 1/2 part neem cake or karanja cake
- 1/4 part kelp meal
- 1/4 part alfalfa meal

Instructions:

Combine all ingredients thoroughly in a large container or on a tarp.

Moisten the mixture until it reaches the consistency of a wrung-out sponge.

Cover the mix and let it sit for a few weeks to allow for nutrient cycling and the establishment of beneficial microorganisms.

Fill your containers or beds with the prepared soil and then plant your seeds.

SUBCOOL SUPER SOIL

The Subcool Super Soil is another well-known organic soil mix used by cannabis growers and developed by a grower named Subcool, the founder of TGA Genetics. This soil mix is designed to provide a rich and fertile growing medium, with the goal of minimizing the need for additional fertilizers during the plant's life cycle. It consists of peat moss, compost, worm castings, aeration inputs, and several organic amendments rich in essential nutrients.

Ingredients:

- 1 part high-quality compost
- 1 part sphagnum peat moss
- 1 part perlite or vermiculite
- 1/2 part worm castings
- 1/2 part bat guano (vegetative)
- 1/2 part fish meal
- 1/2 part kelp meal
- 1/3 part bone meal
- 1/3 part blood meal
- 1/3 part dolomite lime
- 1/3 part Epsom salt

Instructions:

Thoroughly mix all dry ingredients together.

Moisten the mixture until it reaches a damp but not soggy consistency.

Allow the mixture to sit for approximately 30 days, occasionally turning and aerating it.

After the resting period, fill your containers or beds with the prepared soil and then plant your seeds in it.

In addition to the ClackamasCoot Soil Mix and Subcool's Super Soil, there are countless other organic soil recipes that you can find on various internet sources. Experimenting with different recipes can help you understand what works best for your plants and what doesn't. Finding the perfect blend for your cannabis plants may be a challenge, but it can become more manageable if you begin with a well-known soil recipe that has a track record of producing successful results.

CHAPTER 20: FERTILIZERS & AMENDMENTS

FERTILIZERS & *Amendments*

There are numerous organic fertilizers and amendments that you can use in your cannabis garden. Fertilizers play a direct role in enhancing the nutrient content in the soil, which in turn directly impacts plant growth. On the other hand, soil amendments are designed to enhance the soil's physical attributes, such as structure, microbial activity, and water retention. These improvements indirectly influence plant growth. These diverse organic inputs offer a spectrum of nutritional benefits. Some experienced growers prefer using the inputs in this chapter to craft their own custom blend tailored to their specific requirements instead of relying on pre-made fertilizer blends, as discussed in the Base Inputs chapter. However, this approach is not typically recommended for beginners because it requires a careful balance of nutrients to avoid nutrient imbalances that could inhibit plant growth. If you decide to go the custom blend route, it's advisable to conduct a soil test to identify existing nutrient levels in the soil. Once you understand your soil's needs, you can supplement the necessary nutrients using appropriate inputs. If you find comprehending soil test results or determining the correct input amounts challenging, specialized consultants, such as Bryant Mason, known as the Soil Doctor, can provide valuable guidance.

Another approach for utilizing organic inputs is addressing specific nutrient deficiencies in your plants. Growers can incorporate targeted inputs to combat these deficiencies. Below, you'll find a list of essential nutrients and the corresponding organic inputs that can resolve deficiencies in those elements:

- **Nitrogen:** Soy meal, feather meal, kelp meal, blood meal, high-nitrogen bat guano, chicken manure, and fish fertilizer.

- **Phosphorus:** Soft rock phosphate, bone meal, bone char, seabird guano, and rock dust.

- **Potassium:** Compost, langbeinite, greensand, and kelp.

- **Calcium:** Dolomitic lime, garden lime, gypsum, crustacean meal, and oyster shell flour.

- **Magnesium:** Epsom salt and dolomitic lime.

- **Sulfur:** Gypsum and Ag Sulfur.

It's important to note that some of these inputs provide multiple types of nutrients. For example, gypsum supplies both sulfur and calcium. Therefore, if you intend to address a sulfur deficiency but already have an excess of calcium in your soil, gypsum may not be the most suitable choice. Another example, dolomitic lime enriches the soil with both calcium and magnesium. These are just a couple of examples of inputs that offer more than one essential nutrient. In the Base Inputs chapter, we focused on organic fertilizer blends, worm castings, and compost. In this chapter, we will cover 20 other organic fertilizers and amendments, revealing their benefits for your garden and providing general guidance on their application rates.

ALFALFA MEAL

WHAT IS ALFALFA MEAL?

Alfalfa boasts a rich history dating back to the times of the Romans and Babylonians. Initially employed as horse feed, it may come as a surprise that this flowering legume offers equal benefits to your cannabis plants. Alfalfa meal, derived from these resilient perennial plants, undergoes a process of drying, grinding, and fermentation before being pelletized for livestock consumption. Conveniently, you can readily find alfalfa meal as a fertilizer at gardening stores. This organic, plant-based fertilizer delivers a multitude of advantages for the health and growth of your cannabis plants.

Benefits

Alfalfa meal stands as an excellent choice for organic growers, offering a range of benefits to your plants:

- **N-P-K Boost:** Alfalfa meal boasts an N-P-K value close to 3-1-2, providing a rapid boost of nitrogen, phosphorus, and potassium.

- **Other Nutrients:** Beyond being a high-nitrogen fertilizer, alfalfa meal is rich in additional nutrients such as calcium, potassium, sulfur, zinc, boron, and various other essential minerals.

- **Triacontanol:** A unique feature of alfalfa meal is its content of triacontanol, a fatty acid growth hormone. This hormone stimulates root and overall plant growth, proving highly beneficial during the vegetative stage. Additionally, it enhances photosynthesis.

- **Nematode Control:** Alfalfa meal has been proven to suppress harmful nematodes, including root-knot nematodes. It can reduce their populations and even prevent infestations.

🌿 **Moisture Retention:** Alfalfa meal acts as an effective agent for retaining moisture in the soil. It absorbs and holds moisture, offering an additional advantage for plant growth.

These represent some of the primary benefits of alfalfa meal, but the list is by no means complete.

Application

There are several ways to incorporate alfalfa meal into your garden. It's recommended to use alfalfa meal instead of pellets when mixing it into the soil, as pellets can create alfalfa "hot-spots" that may harm cannabis plant roots as they decompose. Here's how to add it to your garden:

🌿 **Top-Dressing:** To use alfalfa meal as a top-dressing, apply it once a month at 1/4 to 1/2 cup per cubic foot. Simply sprinkle it on the soil and work it into the top layer of soil with a rake or your hands. Alternatively, apply mulch on top of it. Then water the plant.

🌿 **Fertilizer Tea:** To create alfalfa fertilizer tea, mix 1 to 2 cups of alfalfa meal in four gallons of water (use a large five-gallon bucket). Let it soak for a day or two; longer soaking results in a stronger tea. Aerating the mixture with air stones or by hand mixing. After proper soaking, strain out the alfalfa and use the tea for foliar or general feeding.

AZOMITE

WHAT IS AZOMITE?

Azomite is a fantastic soil amendment with an interesting history. It originates from an ore mine in Utah, believed to have formed from a volcano that erupted 30 million years ago and settled in a sea bed, resulting in its unique composition. This intricate silica, primarily composed of sodium calcium aluminosilicate (HCAS), earned the registered trademark AZOMITE, which stands for "A to Z of Minerals Including Trace Elements," thanks to Rollin Anderson in the 1940s.

This natural mineral revitalizes the soil by supplying essential micro-nutrients and approximately 75 trace minerals. While most fertilizer programs focus on macronutrients like nitrogen, phosphorus, and potassium, the importance of trace elements often goes overlooked, negatively affecting overall plant health and growth.

Benefits

Azomite offers a number of benefits. Here are some key benefits:

- **Nutrient-Rich:** Azomite contains approximately 75 nutrients that are vital for plant growth. Notably, it contains boron, calcium, and molybdenum.

- **pH Neutral:** One of the wonderful qualities of Azomite is its pH neutrality. This means that when you use Azomite as a soil amendment, it won't disrupt or alter the soil's pH balance.

Application

Azomite is available in several forms and can be applied in various ways. It can be found in ultrafine, micronized, granulated, and pelletized forms. The pelletized form is ideal for slowly releasing nutrients. Azomite can be used as a top-dressing or mixed into the soil.

- **Mixing with Soil:** To use for soil mixing, add 1-2 tablespoons per gallon of soil and mix thoroughly OR add 0.5-1 lb per cubic yard.

- **Top Dressing:** To use as a top dressing, lightly mix 1-2 teaspoons per gallon into the soil surface every other month during the grow cycle.

BAT GUANO

WHAT IS BAT GUANO?

Bat Guano is the term for the manure or feces produced by bats. The word "guano" finds its origins in an ancient South American Quechan word, "wanu," which simply means manure. Bats typically inhabit caves in large colonies, and over time, their excrement accumulates on cave floors, serving as the primary source of Bat Guano fertilizer. These caves are predominantly located in regions such as Mexico, Spain, Peru, India, and Indonesia. Typically, the N-P-K ratio ranges from 8-1-1 to 0-12-0, making it suitable for different growth stages.

Benefits

Bat Guano is a superfood for plants, offering multiple benefits. Here are some reasons to include Bat Guano in your cannabis garden:

- **Nutrients:** Bat Guano is particularly valuable due to its rich content of macronutrients. Notably, it contains high levels of nitrogen, phosphorus, and potassium. Beyond providing macro-nutrients, Bat Guano also provides plants with essential micronutrients. The N-P-K ratio of Bat Guano can vary depending on its source; for example, guano sourced from insect-eating bats is rich in nitrogen, while that from fruit-eating bats is high in phosphorus.

- **Soil Conditioning:** In addition to its nutrient content, Bat Guano functions as a soil conditioner, improving soil texture. It binds loose soil and loosens dense soil, enabling proper water penetration.

Application

There are various ways to incorporate Bat Guano into your cannabis garden:

- **Mixing with Soil:** To use for soil mixing, add 1-2 teaspoons per gallon of soil and mix thoroughly OR add 2.5-5 lbs per cubic yard. Allow the soil to rest for a few days to facilitate the gradual release of nutrients.

🌿 **Top Dressing:** To use as a top dressing, slightly mix 1 teaspoon per gallon into the soil surface once each month during the grow cycle. Water the soil to help it blend effectively.

🌿 **Bat Guano Tea:** Bat Guano can also be used to create a nutrient-rich tea. Add 1-2 tablespoons per gallon of water and let steep up to 48 hours, agitating periodically. Apply the solution directly to the soil around plants and/or apply as a foliar spray. Be sure to use all of the solution once it is prepared.

BLOOD MEAL

WHAT IS BLOOD MEAL?

Blood meal, as the name suggests, is a product derived from the blood collected at slaughterhouses, originating from various livestock destined for human consumption. This blood undergoes processing to transform it into an inert powder, resulting in what we know as blood meal. Different methods are used for drying the blood, including spray drying, oven drying, and solar drying. This natural fertilizer is valued for its high nitrogen content which is in a slow-release form. In addition to containing 13% nitrogen, blood meal also consists of approximately 0.6% potassium and 1% phosphorus.

Benefits

Blood meal, being a natural fertilizer, provides several advantages for plants and soil. Here are some key benefits:

🌿 **Major Macronutrient Source:** Blood meal stands out as an exceptional nitrogen source due to its elevated nitrogen content. Blood meal supplies plants with nitrogen without risk of nutrient burn, thanks to its slow-release nature. It also has some phosphorus and potassium.

🍃 **Waste Reduction:** As blood meal is derived from the by-products or waste of slaughterhouses, its use contributes to waste reduction, benefiting the environment.

Application

Blood meal is readily available at gardening stores and local nurseries. Being water-soluble, it offers flexibility in application methods. Here are some common ways to apply it:

🍃 **Mixing with Soil:** To use for soil mixing, add 1-2 teaspoons per gallon of soil and mix thoroughly.

🍃 **Top Dressing:** To use as a top dressing, lightly mix 1 teaspoon per gallon into the soil surface once each month during the grow cycle.

🍃 **Liquid Fertilizer:** Mix approximately 2 tablespoons of blood meal per gallon of water then use it as a liquid fertilizer for your plants.

One important consideration is that blood meal is a slow-release fertilizer, so it may take a few weeks to observe its full effects after application. While blood meal can deter many pests like deer and rabbits, it may attract certain animals like possums and dogs, so this aspect should also be weighed before using it as a top dressing or soil amendment.

BONE MEAL

WHAT IS BONE MEAL?

Bone meal is an organic fertilizer and soil amendment crafted from bones, typically sourced from slaughterhouse by-products that are unsuitable for consumption. In the bone meal production process, cattle bones undergo steaming or boiling before being finely ground into a powder.

Benefits

The addition of bone meal in cannabis cultivation offers numerous benefits. Here are some key ways in which bone meal benefits both plants and the soil:

- **Phosphorus Source:** Bone meal has a high amount of phosphorus, with an N-P-K ratio of 3-15-0, making it a reliable source of this essential nutrient. Additionally, since it's a slow-release fertilizer, bone meal continues to provide phosphorus to plants for up to four months after application.

- **Calcium Provider:** Bone meal contains approximately 25% calcium which greatly helps meet the needs of cannabis plants.

- **Potential Nitrogen Content:** Bone meal may also contain nitrogen. The slow-release nature of bone meal ensures it doesn't cause nutrient burn and facilitates prolonged nutrient absorption.

Application

When using bone meal for cannabis cultivation, several effective methods are available. However, it's crucial to ensure that the soil's pH is below 7.0, as phosphorus availability to plants is limited in an alkaline root zone. Performing a soil test before application helps determine the suitability of bone meal. Here's how to apply bone meal:

- **Mixing with Soil:** To use for soil mixing, add 1-2 tablespoons per gallon of soil and mix thoroughly OR add 2.5-5 lbs per cubic yard.

- **Top Dressing:** To use as a top dressing, lightly mix 1-2 tablespoons per gallon into the soil surface once each month during the grow cycle.

COTTONSEED MEAL

WHAT IS COTTONSEED MEAL?

Cottonseed meal is a valuable by-product that remains after cotton undergoes processing and its oil is extracted from the seeds. The extraction of cottonseed oil is done in various ways, including mechanical extraction, direct solvent extraction, and pre-press solvent extraction. These methods yield different types of cottonseed meal. Cottonseed meal has an N-P-K ratio of 6-2-2.

Benefits

Cottonseed meal is an excellent organic fertilizer for several reasons:

- **Nutrient Enrichment:** Cottonseed meal is abundant in nitrogen and serves as a valuable source of other essential macronutrients like potassium and phosphorus. Cottonseed meal may also contain trace elements that plants require in smaller quantities.

- **Slow-Release Properties:** Cottonseed meal acts as a slow-release fertilizer, relying on microbial activity to become available to plants. This characteristic minimizes the risk of causing nutrient burn.

- **Water Retention:** Cottonseed meal aids in water retention by effectively holding moisture. Consequently, it serves as an ideal soil amendment for enhancing moisture retention.

- **Soil pH Regulation:** Cottonseed meal can assist in neutralizing soil pH, particularly if the soil is alkaline, by mildly acidifying it.

Application

Cottonseed meal is a slow-release fertilizer, and its effects become noticeable a few weeks after application. It's advisable to assess the soil's pH before applying cottonseed meal. Cottonseed meal is not suitable for creating fertilizer tea as it is not water-soluble. Here are a few ways to apply cottonseed meal to your garden:

- **Mixing with Soil:** To use for soil mixing, add 1-2 tablespoons per gallon of soil and mix thoroughly OR add 5-10 lbs per cubic yard.

- **Top Dressing:** To use as a top dressing, lightly mix 1-2 tablespoons per gallon into the soil surface once each month during the grow cycle.

CRUSTACEAN MEAL

WHAT IS CRUSTACEAN MEAL?

Crustaceans, such as crabs, lobsters, and shrimps, belong to the class of aquatic arthropods known for their hard shells or exoskeletons. Crustacean meal is crafted from these resilient shells, primarily composed of protein, chitin, and calcium phosphate. Through a process involving drying and grinding, these shells are transformed into a fine powder, serving the role of a slow-releasing organic fertilizer. Rich in nitrogen, calcium, phosphorus, and magnesium, crustacean meal not only provides nutrients to cannabis plants but also provides protection against various pests and diseases.

Benefits

Crustacean meal proves highly advantageous for both soil and cannabis plants, offering a nutrient boost and safeguarding against pest infestations. Crustacean meal provides nutrients in a slow-release form without the risk of nutrient burn, making it an exceptional organic fertilizer. Here's how crustacean meal benefits plants:

- **Nutrient Enhancement:** Crustacean meal contains proteins that facilitate the gradual release of nitrogen when used as a fertilizer. Additionally, it contributes a significant calcium boost to plants, with a calcium content of 12%. The inclusion of Calcium Phosphate in crustacean shells makes this meal an excellent source of phosphorus as well. Magnesium is also in crustacean meal, boasting a magnesium content of 1.33%.

- **Pest Protection:** Abundant in arthropod shells, chitin is a prominent component of crustacean meal. Chitin enhances plant immunity, creating resistance to various diseases. Acting as an immunomodulator, it protects cannabis plants against root rot and powdery mildew, triggering enzyme production that combats root-damaging nematodes. Additionally, it acts as a deterrent to pests like snails, slugs, and ants.

Application

Utilizing crustacean meal effectively involves a few distinct methods. Given its slow-release nature, it is advisable to apply it several weeks before planting. Here are the recommended application techniques:

- **Mixing with Soil:** To use for soil mixing, add 1-2 tablespoons per gallon of soil and mix thoroughly OR add 5 lbs per cubic yard.

- **Top Dressing:** To use as a top dressing, lightly mix 1-2 tablespoons per gallon into the soil surface once each month during the grow cycle.

FEATHER MEAL

WHAT IS FEATHER MEAL?

Feather meal, as the name suggests, is derived from poultry feathers. Feathers constitute about 5% of a poultry bird's weight but are typically not consumed for food. These feathers primarily consist of keratin, a protein that doesn't directly benefit plants in its natural form. To make feathers agriculturally useful, they undergo hydrolysis, breaking down the keratin into a protein-rich powder. This transformation turns what might be considered poultry slaughter waste into a valuable source of nitrogen. The feather meal production process involves rendering, pressure cooking, and hydrolyzing, significantly reducing the environmental impact of disposing of feathers. Feather meal has an N-P-K ratio of 13-0-0, making it a potent source of nitrogen.

Benefits

Utilizing feather meal in your garden can result in a handful of benefits. Here are some reasons to include feather meal in your cannabis garden:

- **Nitrogen Content:** Its slow-release nitrogen content, combined with an initial quick nitrogen boost, makes it suitable for early use and nitrogen-depleted soils.

- **Slow Release:** Feather meal's gradual nutrient release ensures it won't cause nutrient burn. It can be incorporated into the soil well in advance of planting, with its effects lasting around six months.

- **Soil Enhancement:** Feather meal contributes to soil structure improvement. It enhances microbial activity, aiding in nutrient breakdown and availability.

- **Waste Reduction:** Since feather meal is a by-product of the poultry industry, it aligns with environmentally friendly practices by reducing waste.

Application

Feather meal is a slow-release fertilizer and isn't water-soluble. Here are a few ways to effectively use feather meal:

- **Mixing with Soil:** To use for soil mixing, add 1-2 tablespoons per gallon of soil and mix thoroughly OR add 5-10 lbs per cubic yard.

- **Top Dressing:** To use as a top dressing, lightly mix 1-2 tablespoons per gallon into the soil surface once each month during the grow cycle.

FISH HYDROLYSATE

WHAT IS FISH HYDROLYSATE?

Fish hydrolysate is a type of fish fertilizer derived from by-catch or fish remnants left behind after processing fish for human consumption. These remnants consist of fish carcasses, entrails, scales, fins, and even meat. Unlike fish emulsions, another commonly available fish-based fertilizer, fish hydrolysate is produced through a cold process, minimizing the use of heat during production. It boasts a lower pH compared to emulsions, preserving a greater quantity of macronutrients, micronutrients, trace minerals, and proteins. This cold process also retains the oils, promoting the growth of soil microbes. The result is a liquid fertilizer with an approximate N-P-K ratio of 2-4-1.

Benefits

Fish-based fertilizers have a long history of use due to their multifaceted benefits. Here's how fish hydrolysate benefits cannabis plants and the soil:

- **Nutrient Boost:** Fish hydrolysate serves as an abundant source of macro and micronutrients essential for plant growth. It is rich in essential primary nutrients such as nitrogen, phosphorus, and potassium, along with secondary nutrients like calcium, magnesium, and iron. This organic fertilizer also supplies cannabis plants with amino acids and growth hormones.

- **Microbial Activity:** Fish hydrolysate significantly enhances microbial activity in the soil. Soil microbes play a pivotal role in breaking down fertilizers, making nutrients accessible to plants. Beneficial bacteria and soil fungi aid in soil aeration through their activities, promoting faster root growth.

Application

Fish hydrolysate is available in liquid or powder form, with liquid being the most common option. The specific instructions for usage can often be found on the bottle or package and may vary slightly depending on the brand. Here are some general application methods for fish hydrolysate:

- **Soil Drench:** Dilute the fish hydrolysate in water as specified on the instructions provided on the product label, then drench soil.

- **Foliar Feeding:** Dilute the fish hydrolysate in water as specified on the instructions provided on the product label, then apply via foliar feeding.

- **Compost:** Incorporating fish hydrolysate into your compost mixture can encourage the growth of beneficial soil bacteria and fungi. As a general guideline, you can typically add about 1/4 to 1/2 cup of fish hydrolysate per cubic yard of compost.

- **Compost Tea:** Fish hydrolysate can also be used to enrich compost tea, providing a valuable boost to the microbial life and nutrient content of the tea, which can then be applied to your plants. A general application is to use around 1 to 2 tablespoons of fish hydrolysate per gallon of water when making compost tea.

FISH MEAL

WHAT IS FISH MEAL?

Fish meal, also known as fish powder, as the name suggests, is derived from the inedible remnants of fish, including leftover fish and bycatch. Typically available in powder or cake form, the utilization of fish meal in agriculture and farming traces its roots back to 800 A.D. Notably, references to the use of fish meal can be found in "The Travels of Marco Polo." The production of fish meal involves a process of drying, pressing, and grinding the fish intended for industrial purposes. Throughout this process, oil and water content are reduced, and preservatives are introduced. Fish meal is primarily used to provide plants with a substantial dose of nitrogen with an N-P-K ratio of approximately 10-6-2.

Benefits

Fish meal is one of the more common organic amendments used in cannabis cultivation. Here are several ways in which fish meal can benefit both your cannabis plants and soil:

- **Macronutrient Boost:** Fish meal contains substantial quantities of nitrogen, potassium, and phosphorus. This makes it an excellent organic fertilizer for enhancing plant macronutrient levels. Fish meal enables slow nutrient release into the soil while also facilitating rapid nitrogen absorption by plants.

- **Micronutrient Enrichment:** In addition to being a rich source of macronutrients, fish meal provides cannabis plants with essential micronutrients.

- **Beneficial Bacteria Promotion:** Fish meal promotes the growth of beneficial bacteria in the soil.

- **Long-Term Storage:** Fish meal has a lengthy shelf life and is resistant to spoilage.

Application

Fish meal is available in powder or cake form and can be added to soil or transformed into a liquid form for a foliar spray. Here are ways to use fish meal in your cannabis garden:

- **Mixing with Soil:** To use for soil mixing, add 1-2 tablespoons per gallon of soil and mix thoroughly OR add 2.5-5 lbs per cubic yard.

- **Top Dressing:** To use as a top dressing, lightly mix 1-2 tablespoons per gallon into the soil surface once each month during the grow cycle. Keep in mind, fish meal can emit a strong odor so it's generally advised to mix it with at least four inches of soil.

- **Foliar Spray:** Fish meal liquid can be used as a foliar spray. Typically, 2 tablespoons of powder are added to 1 gallon of water to create the spray.

GREENSAND

WHAT IS GREENSAND?

Greensand, as the name suggests, is a green-colored sand primarily mined from greenish rocks or sandstone found in marine deposits. The primary component of greensand is Glauconite, a green-tinted mineral composed of potassium, iron, and aluminum silicate. Greensand has a rich history of use in agriculture dating back to ancient times. Interestingly, in ancient Rome, this mineral was used to produce green earth pigment for painting. While it typically has an N-P-K ratio of 0-0-3, this ratio can vary based on the region from which the greensand was sourced.

Benefits

Here's how greensand benefits plants:

- **Potassium Boost:** Greensand provides a valuable source of potassium.

- **Trace Minerals and Other Nutrients:** Beyond potassium, greensand contains up to 30 essential trace minerals, enhancing soil fertility. It also contains iron and silica.

- **Water Retention:** Greensand is excellent at retaining moisture in the soil, promoting consistent hydration for plants. This is particularly beneficial in arid or drought-prone regions where water conservation is essential.

- **Soil Structure:** Whether addressing compacted soil or improving loose, sandy soil, greensand contributes to better soil structure. This can lead to improved root development and aeration for healthier plants.

Application

Greensand typically takes several months to become bioavailable, with an average breakdown period of up to 12 months in the soil. Therefore, it is advisable to incorporate greensand into recycled soil rather than single-use soil. This approach conserves both time and money while ensuring the maximum benefit from greensand. Application rates for greensand fertilizer vary based on usage. In general:

- **Mixing with Soil:** To use for soil mixing, add ¼ to ½ cup of greensand per cubic foot of soil.

- **Transplanting:** When transplanting, use 1 to 2 tablespoons of greensand per gallon of soil.

- **Top Dressing:** To use as a top dressing, lightly mix 1-2 tablespoons per gallon into the soil surface once each month during the grow cycle.

HUMIC ACID

WHAT IS HUMIC ACID?

Humic Acid is a substance that results from the decomposition of organic matter. It's the final stage of decay, where the organic matter can no longer break down further. In more complex terms, the formation of humic acid and humus requires a process called humification. Naturally occurring humic acid can be found in peat moss, marshy water areas, and over some coal deposits, where it's known as Leonardite. Many humic acid products are derived from Leonardite, which can be thought of as a substance that hasn't yet fully turned into coal through carbonization. While the chemical composition of humic acid is intricate, it possesses several properties that benefit plant growth and nutrient availability.

Benefits

There are numerous advantages to using humic acids in cannabis cultivation:

- **Soil Improvement:** Humic acid plays a crucial role in enhancing overall soil structure. It effectively breaks down compacted soil, increases moisture retention due to its high molecular weight, and promotes microbial activity in the soil. These improvements result in healthier soil, stronger root systems, and vigorous plant growth.

- **Nutrient Availability:** Humic acid not only acts as a soil conditioner but also facilitates the availability of various nutrients to plants. It functions as a chelating agent, binding to micronutrients and aiding their transport to the plant. This not only enhances the absorption of micronutrients but also safeguards their availability, preventing depletion.

- **Immobilizes Ions:** Humic acid plays a vital role in minimizing a plant's uptake of sodium, other metals, and toxins. As a natural chelating agent, it forms stable complexes with these harmful elements in the soil. This chelation effectively immobilizes sodium ions, heavy metals, and various toxins, preventing them from being absorbed by plant roots.

Application

Humic acid is available in both powder and liquid forms, offering flexibility in application. For specific usage directions, refer to the instructions provided on the bottle or packaging. As a general guideline, here's how to effectively apply granular humic acid:

- **Mixing with Soil:** To use for soil mixing, add 1-2 teaspoons per gallon of soil and mix thoroughly OR add 1-2 lbs per cubic yard.

- **Transplanting:** For transplanting, use 1-2 teaspoons of humic acid per gallon of soil.

- **Top Dressing:** To use as a top dressing, lightly mix 1-2 teaspoons per gallon into the soil surface every other month during the grow cycle.

- **Foliar Spray:** During the vegetative stage, humic acid can be used as a foliar spray. Dilute in water at a ratio of 1 to 2 teaspoons of granular humic acid per gallon of water, but the specific ratio may vary depending on the product. Stir the mixture thoroughly until the granules dissolve, and then transfer it to a spray bottle or sprayer.

INSECT FRASS

WHAT IS INSECT FRASS?

Insect frass refers to the excrement produced by insects, consisting of both solid droppings and liquid forms. This waste is generated by various insects, including caterpillars, mealworms, and soldier flies. While it's frequently marketed as "frass," specialized products like cricket frass or mealworm castings are also available. Insect frass typically boasts an N-P-K ratio of 2-2-2 and contains additional components such as ammonium, urea, and fatty acids.

Benefits

Insect frass is commonly integrated into cannabis cultivation due to its unique benefits. Here's how insect frass can benefit both the soil and the plants:

- **Chitin:** Insect frass contains chitin, a key component that builds plants' natural defense mechanisms against pests. Chitin serves as a long-term immunity agent by triggering the plant's production of chitinase – an enzyme that breaks down chitin. This process not only increases the plant's immunity but also reinforces its cell walls, promoting rapid growth and heightened resistance to potential threats. Chitin acts as both pest control and a growth enhancer.

- **Beneficial Microbes:** Insect frass promotes the growth of mycorrhizal fungi in the plant's root zone, enhancing nutrient absorption. By providing carbon to these symbiotic fungi, it facilitates their propagation, resulting in a healthier root zone and improved nutrient uptake.

Nutrient Boost: In addition to its N-P-K ratio of 2-2-2, it also contains ammonium, urea, and fatty acids. Some insect frass products may even include insect exoskeletons, which can add calcium to the soil.

Application

There are several application methods for insect frass to consider. These include:

Mixing with Soil: To use for soil mixing, add 1-2 tablespoons per gallon of soil and mix thoroughly OR add 1 cup per cubic foot.

Top Dressing: To use as a top dressing, lightly mix 1-2 tablespoons per gallon into the soil surface once each month during the grow cycle.

Nutrient Tea: To create a nutrient-rich tea extract, mix a ½ cup of insect frass with 1 gallon of water. Allow the solution to steep for approximately 4 hours before using it as a soil drench.

Foliar Feeding: To use as a foliar feed, mix 1-2 teaspoons of insect frass with 1 gallon of water then spray into the leaves.

KELP MEAL

WHAT IS KELP MEAL?

Kelp meal, also referred to as seaweed powder, is an organic fertilizer derived from kelp, a type of seaweed algae. Extensive kelp forests grow in shallow waters near shorelines and they absorb a multitude of nutrients. It's an excellent choice for organic cannabis cultivation due to it being a renewable source and its incredible benefits for cannabis plants. Kelp meal has the ability to fulfill all essential elements required for cannabis plants with an N-P-K ratio of approximately 1-0-2

Benefits

Kelp offers significant advantages for both the soil and cannabis plants. Here's how kelp meal can benefit your garden:

- **Nutrients:** Kelp meal includes all of the macro and micronutrients required for cannabis plants.

- **Trace Minerals:** Kelp meal is a big source for trace elements. It contains over 60 trace elements, including zinc, cobalt, molybdenum, iron, manganese, and more.

- **Moisture Retention:** Kelp meal aids in soil moisture retention, reducing weed intrusion and competing plant growth.

- **Disease Resistance:** Kelp meal increases plants' defenses against viruses and harmful bacteria. Additionally, it promotes the growth of beneficial bacteria and microorganisms, enriching the soil.

- **Growth Stimulation:** Kelp meal contains growth hormones like cytokinin and gibberellins. Cytokinin enhances chlorophyll concentration, while gibberellins facilitate stem elongation, promoting vigorous plant growth.

Application

Kelp meal is available in both powdered and liquid forms. Liquid kelp is typically made from powdered extract and can be used as a foliar spray. Here are four methods for utilizing kelp meal:

- **Mixing with Soil:** To use for soil mixing, add 1-2 tablespoons per gallon of soil and mix thoroughly OR add 2.5 lbs per cubic yard.

- **Top Dressing:** To use as a top dressing, lightly mix 1-2 tsp per gallon into the soil surface once each month during the grow cycle.

- **Foliar Spray:** Mix ½ teaspoons of kelp powder with 5 liters of water to create a kelp foliar spray. Apply this solution directly to the leaves.

- **Liquid Fertilization:** To use liquid kelp, add 2 teaspoons of liquid to 5 liters of water, then water your plants with it.

LANGBEINITE

WHAT IS LANGBEINITE?

Langbeinite, also known as K-Mag or Sul-Po-Mag, is a natural mineral fertilizer primarily found in mines located in New Mexico, USA. These deposits originate from the evaporation of ancient oceanic beds. The mineral's chemical composition consists of potassium, magnesium, and sulfate. It was commercialized in the 1930s and is extracted using drilling machines. Langbeinite has a neutral pH and adding it to the soil does not affect its pH. Langbeinite has an approximate N-P-K ratio of 0-0-22.

Benefits

Langbeinite offers several benefits to both soil and plants. Here are some key benefits:

- **Potassium Source:** Langbeinite is a valuable source of potassium, which contributes to denser buds and increased yield during the plant's flowering stage.

- **Magnesium Content:** While not a macronutrient, magnesium in langbeinite supports photosynthesis by aiding chlorophyll production, giving plants their green color.

- **Sulfur Inclusion:** Langbeinite contains sulfur, crucial for terpene and cannabinoid production, as well as nutrient metabolism and uptake.

- **Neutral pH:** Langbeinite maintains a neutral pH, preventing disruptions in soil chemistry and avoiding issues like nutrient lockouts or pH imbalances.

- **Water Solubility:** Its water-soluble which results in nutrient availability to plants when mixed in water.

- **Root System Enhancement:** Potassium strengthens root systems, making plants more resistant to diseases, pests, drought, and adverse weather conditions.

Safe for Sensitive Plants: Suitable for plants like cannabis that are sensitive to chlorine or salt, making it a safe choice for cultivation.

Application

Langbeinite can be mixed into soil before planting, can be added as a top dressing to existing plants, or be mixed into water and then used as a soil drench. Although langbeinite is water-soluble, it may take some time to dissolve due to its particle size. Using lukewarm water can expedite the particles getting into solution.

- **Soil Drench:** To use as soil drench, mix 1-2 tablespoons per gallon of water, then water your plants with it.

- **Mixing with Soil:** To use for soil mixing, mix 1 tablespoon per gallon of soil and mix thoroughly OR add 1-2 lbs per cubic yard.

- **Top Dressing:** To use as a top dressing, lightly mix 1-2 teaspoons per gallon into the soil surface once each month during the grow cycle.

- **Foliar Spray:** For a foliar spray application, mix ½-1 teaspoon per gallon of water.

NEEM SEED MEAL

WHAT IS NEEM SEED MEAL?

Neem seed meal, as the name suggests, is derived from the neem tree, which is native to South Asia. This tree thrives in countries such as India, Sri Lanka, Bangladesh, and neighboring regions. Neem is found in various products, including cosmetics, and the primary source of neem "oil" comes from neem seeds. When neem seeds are pressed for oil extraction, the residual material becomes neem seed meal. Neem has numerous benefits, and the same holds true for neem seed meal. Not only does it provide a nutrient boost, but it also promotes microbial growth and serves as a natural pest control solution. Neem seed meal has a N-P-K ratio of 6-1-2.

Benefits

Neem seed meal offers significant advantages for cannabis plants and the soil. Here's how neem seed meal can increase soil quality and promote plant growth:

- **Nutrient Boost:** Neem seed meal is rich in macronutrients nitrogen, phosphorus, and potassium. It is also a rich source of micronutrients.

- **Pest Control:** Neem seed meal not only encourages the growth of beneficial microbes but also acts as a natural deterrent for parasites. It enhances soil activity while repelling harmful organisms such as mites, aphids, thrips, snails and grasshoppers. The presence of azadirachtin in neem helps kill off these pests, functioning as a natural pesticide.

Application

Neem seed meal can be effectively integrated into your feeding routine through various methods. Here are some recommended ways to use neem seed meal:

- **Mixing with Soil:** To use for soil mixing, add ⅛ – ¼ cup per gallon of soil and mix thoroughly OR add 5-10 lbs per cubic yard.

- **Top Dressing:** To use as a top dressing, lightly mix 2-4 tablespoons per gallon into the soil surface once each month during the grow cycle.

- **Neem Seed Meal Tea:** Soak two cups of neem seed meal in a gallon of water, preferably using a mesh bag and adding air stones to the water bucket. The tea typically takes 48 hours to be ready and can be used as a soil drench or as a foliar spray.

OYSTER SHELL

WHAT IS OYSTER SHELL?

Oyster shells, often found along ocean shores, are the durable exoskeletons of oysters, classified as mollusks. These shells predominantly inhabit saltwater environments and are primarily composed of calcium carbonate. Oysters utilize the lime in water to construct their shells, a process that keeps these mollusks hydrated and results in shells rich in calcium. This makes oyster shells an excellent slow-release fertilizer for plants.

Benefits

Oyster shells offer several advantages as a slow-release organic fertilizer, benefiting plants in multiple ways. Here are some key ways in which oyster shells benefit plant growth:

- **Nutrient Boost:** Oyster shells are an excellent source of calcium, magnesium, iron, sodium, and various other micronutrients.

- **pH Buffer:** Oyster shells can function as a pH buffer, helping to regulate soil pH. In cases where the soil is overly alkaline, oyster shells can assist in restoring it to an optimal level.

- **Pest Control:** Oyster shells have pest-repelling properties, deterring pests such as moles, slugs, and snails.

- **Aeration and Drainage:** Crushed oyster shells create a coarse texture, helping improve soil aeration and drainage.

Application

Crushed oyster shells break down slowly, providing a longer-lasting release of calcium to the soil. Here are a few common ways that oyster shells can be added to your garden:

- **Mixing with Soil:** To use for soil mixing, add 1-2 tablespoons per gallon of soil and mix thoroughly OR add 0.5-1 lb per cubic yard.

- **Top Dressing:** To use as a top dressing, lightly mix 1-2 tablespoons per gallon into the soil surface every other month during the grow cycle.

ROCK PHOSPHATE

WHAT IS ROCK PHOSPHATE?

Rock phosphate, also known as phosphorite or phosphate rock, is a sedimentary rock extracted from various mineral deposits located in shallow and near-shore environments. Countries with substantial rock phosphate reserves include the United States, China, Russia, and Morocco. Rock phosphate typically contains phosphorus levels ranging from 4% to 20%, but beneficiation processes can increase concentrations to around 28%. Rock phosphate has a N-P-K ratio of 0-3-0.

Benefits

Rock phosphate is a slow-release fertilizer that provides numerous advantages to plants, their root systems, and the soil. Here's how rock phosphate benefits plants:

- **Phosphorus Boost:** Rock phosphate is an excellent source of phosphorus. Additionally, it provides secondary nutrients like calcium.

- **Root Growth:** The phosphorus from rock phosphate enhances the root zone, promoting the development of large and resilient root systems.

- **Pest and Disease Resistance:** Phosphorus strengthens plants, making them more resistant to pests and capable of thriving in challenging conditions such as frost or drought.

Application

A single application of this slow-release fertilizer can continue to benefit plants over an extended period. Soil pH should be checked before adding rock phosphate, as it is most effective in slightly acidic conditions with a pH below 5.5. Application is recommended well in advance of planting.

- **Mixing with Soil:** To use for soil mixing, add ¼ cup per gallon of soil and mix thoroughly OR add 5-10 lbs per cubic yard.

- **Top Dressing:** To use as a top dressing, lightly mix 1 tablespoon per gallon into the soil surface every other month during the grow cycle.

SEABIRD GUANO

WHAT IS SEABIRD GUANO?

Seabird guano has been used as a fertilizer for centuries due to its abundance of essential nutrients. The term "guano" originates from the Quencha language and simply refers to bird or bat excrement. Typically consisting of the manure or waste of birds and bats, seabird guano, often dubbed the "white gold of the sea," has a rich history dating back to the Incas, who were among the first to recognize its agricultural benefits. Nutrients included are calcium, potassium, molybdenum, iron, and manganese. Seabird guano offers the benefits of a slow-release, long-term fertilizer that supplies both micro and macronutrients to plants. While nutrient composition can vary depending on the guano's source, most packaged seabird guano fertilizers boast an N-P-K ratio of 1-10-1, with high-nitrogen variants featuring an N-P-K ratio of approximately 12-18-1.

Benefits

Seabird guano delivers substantial benefits to plants, despite its potential higher cost compared to other natural fertilizers. Its advantages include:

- **Nutrient Boost:** Seabird guano, available in varying N-P-K compositions, provides plants with essential macronutrients required for daily functions.

- **Slow-Release Fertilizer:** Seabird guano acts as a slow-release, organic soil amendment that does not pose a risk of burning plants. It takes approximately four months for the nutrients in seabird guano to become available to plants.

- **Microbial Activity:** Seabird guano accelerates biological activity within the soil, stimulating microbial populations and improving soil structure.

Application

Seabird guano is typically offered in powder or pelletized forms. Here are some ways to apply it to your garden:

- **Soil Drench:** Mix 1-2 tablespoons of seabird guano with 1 gallon of water and allow it to steep for two days, then water your plants with it.

- **Mixing with Soil:** To use for soil mixing, add 1-2 tablespoons per gallon of soil and mix thoroughly OR add 2.5-5 lbs per cubic yard.

- **Top Dressing:** To use as a top dressing, lightly mix 1 tablespoon per gallon into the soil surface once each month during the grow cycle.

- **Foliar Spray:** Mix 1-2 tablespoons of seabird guano with 1 gallon of water and allow it to steep for two days, then spray your plants with it.

SOYBEAN MEAL

WHAT IS SOYBEAN MEAL?

Soybean, a versatile edible legume utilized in various human food products, also serves as a component in animal feed and organic, plant-based fertilizers. Soybean meal is a by-product of soybean oil production. Its high protein content makes it a staple in animal feed, and it's equally valued as a fertilizer due to its nitrogen content. While soybean meal functions effectively as a multi-purpose fertilizer, its affordability and availability make it particularly attractive. Soybean meal has an N-P-K ratio of 7-1-2.

Benefits

Despite its cost-effectiveness and widespread availability, soybean meal offers substantial benefits to plants. Here are some reasons to include soybean meal in your cannabis garden:

- **Nutrient Enrichment:** Soybean meal contains 7% nitrogen, 2% phosphorus, and 1% potassium, ensuring a comprehensive macronutrient supply to plants.

- **Microbial Activity and Soil Improvement:** Soybean meal encourages the proliferation of beneficial soil microbes, which aid in its decomposition and the subsequent release of nutrients. This boost in microbial populations enhances soil structure and overall soil health.

- **Organic and Plant-Based:** Soybean meal serves as a slow-release organic fertilizer, posing no risk of nutrient burn. It's an environmentally-friendly choice as it derives from the by-products of soybean oil extraction, making it ideal for those seeking plant-based organic fertilizers.

🍁 **Neutral pH:** Soybean meal maintains a relatively neutral pH level, making it an excellent choice for supplying nutrients to plants without affecting soil acidity.

Application

Soybean meal is available in powdered form and is not water-soluble. Here are a few common ways that soybean meal can be added to your garden:

🍁 **Mixing with Soil:** To use for soil mixing, add 2-4 tablespoons per gallon of soil and mix thoroughly OR add 2.5-5 lbs per cubic yard.

🍁 **Top Dressing:** To use as a top dressing, lightly mix 1-2 tablespoons per gallon into the soil surface once each month during the grow cycle.

CHAPTER 21: DIY FERTILIZERS

DIY Fertilizers

Instead of buying a variety of fertilizers from the store, you can make them yourself using items you probably already have at home. Many gardeners are turning to household items like eggshells, banana peels, fruits, and even plant material to create their own DIY (do-it-yourself) fertilizers. It's not only a sustainable way to repurpose items that might otherwise end up in the trash but also a rewarding way to enrich your soil with nutrients and beneficial microorganisms.

In this chapter, we will explore a range of DIY gardening fertilizers. Before we dive into specific recipes and techniques, let's take a closer look at the many advantages of DIY gardening.

Benefits

There are many advantages for creating your own DIY fertilizers. Here is a small handful of benefits:

- **Cost-Effective:** One of the primary advantages of DIY gardening is cost savings. Commercial fertilizers and soil amendments can be expensive, especially if you have a large garden. By making your own, you'll not only save money but also reduce your reliance on store-bought products.

- **Environmental Friendliness:** Many commercial fertilizers contain chemicals that can harm the environment. DIY fertilizers typically involve using natural, organic materials that are less harmful to the planet. It's an eco-conscious way to nurture your garden.

- **Sustainability:** DIY gardening often involves recycling kitchen scraps and waste materials, promoting sustainability by reducing waste and repurposing resources.

Now, let's move on to the specific DIY fertilizer processes.

EGGSHELLS CALCIUM FERTILIZER

Eggshells are a fantastic source of calcium, which is essential for strong cell walls and healthy root development in plants. Here's how to make a water-soluble calcium fertilizer using eggshells:

Materials:

- Coffee grinder or rolling pin and wooden cutting board
- Small bowl
- Measuring cup with a spout
- Clean, empty gallon jug (a plastic milk jug works fine)
- Wide-mouth jar or container with a lid
- 10 eggshells (or more)
- White vinegar
- 1 gallon of water (rainwater, distilled, or filtered water is best)

Steps:

- **Rinse Eggshells:** Begin by rinsing your eggshells with cool water. Don't worry if they still have some egg white residue or membrane.

- **Put in Oven:** Lay the washed eggshells in a single layer on a baking sheet and dry them in the oven for about 2 hours at its lowest setting, usually around 180°F (85°C). There's no need to preheat the oven.

- **Let them Cool:** Once the eggshells have dried, remove them from the oven and let them cool.

- **Crush Eggshells:** Break the eggshells into smaller pieces using your fingers. You can then use a coffee grinder to crush them into a fine powder. Alternatively, you can use a rolling pin on a wooden cutting board to pulverize the shells.

Storage Container: Place the crushed eggshells in the wide-mouth container. This container can be used to store any extra eggshell powder you don't use right away.

Measure Eggshell Powder: Measure out 2 tablespoons of eggshell powder for every gallon of water you plan to use for your plants and place it in the bowl.

Add Vinegar and Stir: Add an equal amount of white vinegar to the crushed shells. Stir the mixture with a non-metal utensil to allow the vinegar and eggshells to react; you'll notice some bubbling.

Let It React: Let the mixture sit for a minute or two, then give it another good stir. Allow the vinegar and eggshells to react for about an hour.

Transfer Solution: Transfer 4 tablespoons of the eggshell/vinegar solution into a spouted measuring cup, and add some water to make it easier to pour.

Fill the Gallon Jug: Pour the solution into the gallon jug, then fill it almost to the top with water. Secure the jug's lid and shake it well.

Apply to Plants: Fill your watering can from the gallon jug, and use your calcium-rich eggshell fertilizer to water your plants!

BANANA PEELS POTASSIUM FERTILIZER

Potassium is crucial for overall plant health, aiding in photosynthesis, water uptake, and disease resistance. Bananas are rich in potassium and the peels can be used to make a simple fertilizer:

Materials:

- 3-4 banana peels
- A glass jar with a lid
- Water (preferably rainwater, distilled, or filtered water)

Steps:

- **Preparation of Banana Peels:** Start by collecting 3-4 banana peels. If you prefer, you can cut the banana peels into smaller pieces.

- **Jar Placement:** Take your clean glass jar and ensure it's free of any contaminants. It's important to have a clean container to prevent any unwanted growth of microorganisms. Place the banana peels inside the jar.

- **Water Addition:** Fill the jar with water, ensuring that the water covers the banana peels entirely. The choice of water is important - using rainwater, distilled water, or filtered water is preferable as it avoids the introduction of impurities or chlorine that might interfere with the fermentation process. Make sure to use enough water so that the banana peels are fully submerged.

- **Sealing the Jar:** Seal the glass jar with a lid. It's essential to secure the lid tightly to create an airtight environment within the jar. This helps to maintain a stable environment for the fermentation process and prevents any unwanted odors from escaping.

🌿 **Fermentation Period:** Allow the banana peels to soak in the water for approximately a week. During this time, the potassium and other nutrients from the peels will leach into the water, creating a liquid fertilizer.

🌿 **Peel Removal:** Once the soaking period is complete, remove the banana peels from the jar.

🌿 **Fertilizer Application:** Your potassium-rich banana peel fertilizer is now ready for use. You can either water your plants with it as is or further dilute it down in water at a 1:4 ratio.

FERMENTED PLANT JUICE & FERMENTED FRUIT JUICE

Fermented Plant Juice (FPJ) and Fermented Fruit Juice (FFJ) are both exceptional sources of nutrients and growth hormones for your plants. FPJ is typically used during the vegetative stage, while FFJ takes the spotlight when your plants are in full bloom. Here's how to make them:

Materials:

- A glass jar or a food-grade plastic container
- A sharp, clean knife for chopping the biomass
- Organic brown sugar
- A breathable cloth to serve as a "lid" (cheesecloth or nut milk bags are suitable choices)
- Plant material or fruit

Steps:

Collecting Plant Material or Fruit: For FPJ, aim to harvest your plant biomass before the sun rises. Snip the young, vigorously growing tips of your chosen plant, then store them in a clean container. This timing ensures the plants are in a respiration mode, not photosynthesis mode. Avoid collecting during or after heavy rainfall. For FFJ, use fruits that best suit your plants needs for the stage of growth they are in. Additionally, it's important to use ripe or slightly unripe fruits, as they have higher sugar content, which aids in the fermentation process.

Cutting and Weighing the Material: Preserve microorganisms by not rinsing the collected plant parts or fruit. Record the weight of the biomass.

- **Adding Brown Sugar:** Maintain a 1:1 ratio of brown sugar to plant biomass or fruit. For example, if you have one pound of plant material or fruit, add one pound of brown sugar. Ensure the brown sugar coats as much of the surface area of the plant material or fruit as possible to stimulate the fermentation process.

- **Packing the Brown Sugar-Coated Biomass:** Place the brown sugar-coated biomass into a glass jar, ensuring it's packed tightly.

- **Attaching a Breathable Lid:** Secure a breathable lid to the container using string or a rubber band, depending on the jar's size.

- **Storing the Covered Container:** Place the covered container in a well-ventilated area, away from direct light, extreme heat, or cold.

- **Checking After 24 Hours:** After 24 hours, inspect the container and adjust the volume if needed. The jar should not be filled more than 2/3 full, as overfilling may limit the microbes' access to the air required for proper fermentation.

- **Let it Ferment for 4 - 7 Days:** Fermentation is evident when bubbles form in the liquid. It's considered complete when the plant material or fruit floats, the liquid settles at the bottom, and there's a faint alcoholic aroma due to the breakdown of chlorophyll. The liquid should be sweet, not bitter. These are approximate guidelines, as the process can be influenced by the ambient temperature.

- **Straining the Solution:** Separate the plant material or fruit from the liquid. The biomass can be added to compost or mulched directly into your soil.

- **Storage:** Transfer the FPJ or FFJ into a clean glass jar or food-grade plastic container. Cover it with a loose lid, as the microorganisms in the solution remain active and continue to produce carbon dioxide. A tightly sealed lid may lead to pressure build-up.

- **Diluting the FPJ or FFJ:** Dilute at a ratio of 1:500, 1:800, or 1:1,000, which translates to 4-8ml of the juice per gallon of water.

- **Applying the FPJ or FFJ:** You can use the diluted FPJ or FFJ as a soil drench or a foliar spray. Apply the solution once a week - no more frequently than that.

While the DIY fertilizer recipes discussed here are just a small selection of the many available, they serve as a helpful introduction. Incorporating DIY fertilizers into your garden offers numerous benefits. It not only promotes healthier plants but also leads to cost savings and a reduction in waste. Feel free to experiment with these techniques at your own pace, and you'll witness your garden thriving in no time!

CHAPTER 22: COMMON PROBLEMS & SOLUTIONS

COMMON PROBLEMS & *Solutions*

I said it in my previous book, and I'll say it again in this one: I hope you never have to read this chapter. When you're growing cannabis and your plants are thriving, you're happy. On the other hand, encountering problems can lead to frustration and a loss of motivation. Just like nearly every other task, growing cannabis has its fair share of challenges. In this chapter, we will dive into the five most common issues organic cannabis cultivators face and provide solutions to help you overcome them.

PROBLEM 1: PEST INFESTATIONS

Pest infestations are a common challenge for organic cannabis growers. Without implementing Integrated Pest Management practices, you may come across various pests that can harm your plants. While we've already covered the top five common pests in the Pest Prevention chapter, below is a quick summary of actions you can take to combat infestations:

- **Regular Inspection:** Make inspecting your cannabis plants a routine practice. Look for signs of pests, such as white spots on leaves, webbing, or holes. Early detection enables quicker intervention.

- **Beneficial Insects:** Introducing natural predators like ladybugs, lacewings, and predatory mites to your garden can help control pest populations by preying on them.

- **Neem Oil:** Neem oil is an organic insecticide that disrupts pests' feeding and reproductive cycles. To create a spray, mix neem oil with water and a few drops of dish soap. Apply it to the affected plants, ensuring complete coverage of both sides of the leaves.

- **Insecticidal Soaps:** Organic insecticidal soaps are gentle on plants but effective against soft-bodied insects like aphids. Follow the product's instructions for application, and ensure thorough coverage.

- **Other Organic Sprays:** Explore organic sprays such as pyrethrin-based products or homemade solutions like peppermint and rosemary sprays. These can act as deterrents or disrupt pests upon contact.

🍁 **Companion Planting:** Plant companion crops like marigolds, basil, or garlic near your cannabis plants. These can deter or confuse pests with their scents and help reduce infestations.

🍁 **Isolation:** If you suspect an infestation, consider isolating the affected plant to prevent the pests from spreading to other plants. This is especially crucial in indoor growing environments.

🍁 **Crop Rotation:** When growing outdoors, employ crop rotation to reduce the buildup of pests in the soil. Avoid planting cannabis in the same spot in consecutive seasons.

Remember that maintaining a healthy growing environment is essential for pest prevention. Strong, thriving plants are less susceptible to infestations, so focus on proper nutrition, watering, and overall plant care. For more information on preventing and overcoming pest infestations, read the Pest Prevention chapter and Beneficial Insects chapter.

PROBLEM 2: NUTRIENT DEFICIENCIES

Nutrient deficiencies can be a common issue in organic cannabis cultivation. This primarily occurs because organic inputs require time to break down and convert into a form that the plant can readily absorb. Additionally, if you incorporate organic inputs randomly without a clear understanding of their nutrient content, you may inadvertently create imbalances or deficiencies. Also, an excess of some elements can inhibit the uptake of others, resulting in visible signs of nutrient deficiencies. Below is a list of actions you can take to address nutrient deficiencies.

🍁 **Observation and Diagnosis:** Familiarize yourself with the early symptoms of nutrient deficiencies. Keep an eye out for leaf discoloration, yellowing, and unusual growth patterns, as these can indicate nutrient issues.

- **Organic Fertilizers:** Organic growers should choose fertilizers that offer a balanced mix of essential nutrients. Follow the recommended application rates and frequency mentioned on the packaging.

- **Compost Tea:** Compost tea is a nutrient-rich liquid produced by steeping compost in water. It contains various beneficial microorganisms and nutrients that can help rectify deficiencies and enhance soil health.

- **Worm Castings:** Worm castings serve as a natural source of nutrients and beneficial microorganisms. Apply them as a top dressing to provide a slow-release nutrient supply.

- **Mulching:** Utilize organic materials such as straw, leaves, or wood chips as mulch to aid in retaining soil moisture and regulating temperature. As the mulch decomposes, it enriches the soil with valuable organic matter.

- **pH Management:** Ensure that your soil's pH falls within the optimal range for nutrient uptake, which typically ranges between 6.0 and 7.0 for soil. You can adjust the pH with organic amendments such as dolomite lime for alkaline conditions or sulfur for acidic conditions.

- **Regular Soil Testing:** Conduct routine soil tests to monitor nutrient levels and pH. These tests allow you to make informed decisions regarding the addition of organic inputs.

- **Foliar Feeding:** In cases of severe deficiencies, consider foliar feeding. For example, epsom salt mixed into water is often used to help with magnesium deficiency. Spray the solution directly to the leaves to provide a rapid nutrient boost.

Remember that organic cultivation involves the gradual building and maintenance of healthy soil over time. While the effects of organic amendments may take longer to see compared to synthetic fertilizers, the long-term benefits for soil health and sustainability are well worth the effort. Consistent monitoring and proactive nutrient management are essential for a successful organic cannabis garden.

PROBLEM 3: OVERWATERING OR UNDERWATERING

Achieving the right balance of water for your cannabis plants is fundamental to successful cultivation. Both overwatering and underwatering can have adverse effects on plant growth. Below, we'll explore the consequences of these issues and offer tips on maintaining the proper moisture level for your cannabis plants.

Overwatering can harm your cannabis plants in several ways:

- **Root Rot:** Overwatered soil lacks oxygen, creating an environment where harmful fungi thrive. This can lead to wilting, yellowing leaves, and ultimately, plant death.

- **Nutrient Leaching:** Excessive watering can wash away essential nutrients from the soil, resulting in nutrient deficiencies.

- **Stunted Growth:** Overwatered plants often experience slowed growth due to stress and reduced nutrient uptake.

Conversely, underwatering can also damage your cannabis plants:

- **Stunted Growth:** Insufficient water restricts nutrient absorption and photosynthesis, leading to slow growth.

- **Wilting and Drooping:** Underwatered plants exhibit wilting and drooping leaves, clear signs of stress.

- **Nutrient Concentration:** When water is scarce, nutrients can become concentrated in the soil, potentially causing nutrient burn.

- **Reduced Yields:** Chronic underwatering can lead to reduced bud development and smaller yields.

To maintain the proper moisture level for your cannabis plants, follow these guidelines:

- **Check Soil Moisture:** Use a moisture meter for precise measurements. If you're hand watering without a meter, insert your finger about an inch into the soil. If it feels dry at this depth, it's time to water. If it's still moist, wait a bit longer.

- **Ensure Proper Drainage:** Confirm that your containers or garden beds have adequate drainage to prevent water from accumulating at the roots.

- **Apply Mulch:** Add a layer of organic mulch around your plants to help retain soil moisture and regulate temperature.

Finding the right balance in watering practices may require some trial and error. Over time, you'll become more aware of when and how much to water, enabling you to maintain an optimal moisture level. For more in-depth information on proper watering techniques, read the Water chapter.

PROBLEM 4: PH IMBALANCES

Maintaining the correct pH level in your cannabis garden is crucial for ensuring proper nutrient absorption and overall plant health. The pH scale measures the acidity or alkalinity of a substance, with 7.0 being neutral. Cannabis plants thrive in a slightly acidic to neutral pH range. Soil that becomes too acidic (below 6.0) or excessively alkaline (above 7.0) can impact nutrient availability, as certain nutrients become less accessible to the plant outside of this optimal pH range. Even if there are adequate nutrients in the medium at the proper ratios, an imbalanced pH can lead to nutrient deficiencies, which can stunt plant growth and compromise yields.

While some organic gardeners claim they don't monitor pH levels and their plants grow just fine, others encounter issues when pH falls outside the optimal range. Below are some solutions for addressing pH imbalances in your soil should you encounter any issues.

- **Regular pH Testing:** Invest in a reliable pH meter or pH testing kit to regularly monitor the pH of your soil or growing medium. This practice allows you to promptly detect and address pH imbalances. When watering your plants, collect and test the runoff water. Ideally, it should have a pH similar to your target pH, indicating that the soil's pH is well-balanced.

- **pH Adjustment:** Depending on your soil's pH, you may need to adjust it using organic amendments. Common pH adjusters include:

    - **Dolomite Lime (for low pH):** This organic amendment helps raise pH levels in acidic soils gradually over time.

    - **Sulfur (for high pH):** Sulfur can lower pH in alkaline soils, although it acts more slowly than lime.

- **Boost Buffering Capacity:** Enhance your soil's buffering capacity by incorporating organic matter such as compost or worm castings. Additionally, consider using organic materials like humic acid, which can effectively stabilize pH fluctuations in the soil. This practice contributes to the maintenance of a stable pH level over time.

- **Maintain a pH Log:** Keep a record of your pH measurements and any adjustments you make. This log will help you identify trends and adapt your cultivation practices accordingly.

It's important to note that pH management in organic cultivation may require patience, as various factors, including microbes, plants releasing acids, and the inputs you add in, can influence soil pH. Regular monitoring, testing, and a willingness to adapt your approach will help you maintain the ideal pH level for your cannabis plants.

PROBLEM 5: NUTRIENT BURN

Nutrient burn, commonly referred to as fertilizer burn, is a common issue faced by both beginner and experienced cannabis growers. It occurs when the grower provides more nutrients than the plants can effectively absorb, resulting in a buildup of nutrients in the soil that can lead to toxicity. The telltale signs include the browning or yellowing of leaf tips and edges, giving them a burnt appearance. If you encounter this problem, refer to the solutions below to help restore your plant to a healthy state.

Solutions:

- **Follow Feeding Guidelines:** Adhere to the recommended dosage and schedule provided by the manufacturer of your chosen organic fertilizers. In organic cultivation, remember that "less is often more," especially when it comes to nutrient application.

- **Check and Monitor pH Level:** Ensure that your growing medium's pH falls within the optimal range, typically around 6.0 to 7.0 for soil. pH imbalances can affect nutrient uptake, contributing to nutrient burn.

- **Flush:** If symptoms worsen, consider flushing the soil with plain, pH-balanced water. This process helps remove excess nutrients from the soil, mitigating nutrient buildup.

Nutrient burn is a preventable issue that can be effectively managed through careful attention to nutrient application and overall plant health. By closely monitoring your plants and adjusting your feeding schedule as needed, you can minimize the risk of nutrient burn.

EPILOGUE

A As we come to the end of this book on organic cannabis cultivation, I want to congratulate you.

Implementing organic gardening practices, as outlined in this book, demonstrates your commitment to valuing the ecosystem, minimizing negative impacts on the earth, and working with nature rather than against it. With the information provided, you now have the tools to successfully grow organically, and I truly hope your future harvests meet or exceed your expectations.

It's important to keep in mind that this book covers only the basics and some intermediate aspects of organic cultivation. There is always more to learn beyond these pages. I encourage you to challenge yourself to continue learning and improving, as there is endless room for growth.

If you have any questions or simply want to share the progress of your garden, feel free to post on my website's forum. It's not just me answering questions there; a community of knowledgeable growers also participates, providing valuable insights into organic gardening practices.
Visit: www.mrgrowit.com/forum

Lastly, stay connected with me on YouTube, Facebook, Instagram, and Twitter @MrGrowIt for grow videos, pictures, articles, and the latest updates.

Happy growing,
-Mr. Grow It

GLOSSARY

Aerobic - Living, active, or occurring only in the presence of oxygen.

Allelopathic - A biological phenomenon where a plant releases chemicals into its environment, inhibiting the growth or development of nearby competing plants, often as a competitive strategy for resources.

Anaerobic - Living, active, occurring, or existing in the absence of free oxygen.

Antagonistic - When two or more chemicals combine to produce a chemical with a total effect that is less than the sum of the effects of each individual chemical. In simple words, one chemical reduces the effect of another chemical.

Auto-flowering cannabis - A variety of cannabis plants that automatically transition from the vegetative stage to the flowering stage based on age rather than changes in light cycles.

Bioaccumulator - A plant that is capable of absorbing and accumulating certain substances, such as heavy metals or pollutants, from the environment in higher concentrations than those present in the surrounding soil or air.

Bioavailable - In a form that can be easily absorbed and utilized by plants.

Coco coir - A natural fiber extracted from the husk of coconuts, commonly used as a growing medium in horticulture and gardening.

Compost - A nutrient-rich, organic matter that results from the decomposition of biodegradable waste materials, such as kitchen scraps and yard waste, through the action of microorganisms.

Ecosystem - A complex and interconnected community of living organisms (plants, animals, and microorganisms) interacting with each other and their physical environment, forming a dynamic and self-sustaining ecological unit.

Fermented Fruit Juice (FFJ) - A natural liquid fertilizer produced by fermenting the juice extracted from fruits, typically mixed with sugar and water.

Fermented Plant Juice (FPJ) - A natural liquid fertilizer made by fermenting the juice extracted from various plants, often combined with sugar, to enhance nutrient content and microbial activity.

Fertilizer - A substance or mixture containing essential nutrients, such as nitrogen, phosphorus, and potassium, applied to soil or plants to enhance their growth and productivity by providing necessary elements for optimal development.

Flowering stage - A specific phase during which the plant produces and develops flowers.

Fluorescent grow lights - Artificial lighting systems that use fluorescent tubes to provide a spectrum of light suitable for promoting plant growth, particularly during the vegetative stages.

Growing medium - Also known as a substrate, is a material used to support the growth of plants in gardening, horticulture, or hydroponics.

High-Intensity Discharge (HID) grow lights - Powerful artificial lighting systems commonly used in indoor gardening that consist of metal halide and high-pressure sodium lights, providing a high-intensity and broad spectrum of light suitable for various stages of plant growth.

Inert - Does not chemically react with or alter the composition. For example, an inert growing medium is a neutral substrate that allows growers to have precise control over nutrient inputs.

Integrated Pest Management (IPM) - A process that combines tools and strategies for managing and preventing pest infestations.

Light-Emitting Diode (LED) grow lights - Artificial lighting systems that use Light-Emitting Diodes (LEDs) to provide the necessary spectrum of light for plant growth.

Light cycle - Refers to the ratio of light-on to light-off time.

Macronutrients - Essential elements required in large amounts.

Microbial inoculant - Beneficial microorganisms applied either to the soil or the plant to enhance productivity and plant health.

Micronutrients - Essential elements required in small amounts.

Microorganisms - Often referred to as microbes, are microscopic living organisms such as bacteria, viruses, fungi, and protozoa.

Mineralization - The process in which organic matter, such as plant or animal residues, is decomposed by microorganisms into inorganic mineral nutrients like nitrogen, phosphorus, and potassium, making them available for absorption by plants.

Mycorrhizal fungi - Symbiotic fungi that form a mutualistic association with the roots of most plants.

N-P-K ratio - Represents the proportion of nitrogen (N), phosphorus (P), and potassium (K) in the fertilizer.

Organic - Anything derived from living organisms or produced using natural processes without the use of synthetic chemicals or additives.

PAR (Photosynthetically Active Radiation) - The portion of the electromagnetic spectrum, typically between 400 to 700 nanometers, that is crucial for photosynthesis in plants.

Peat moss - A type of organic material derived from partially decomposed sphagnum moss and other plant matter that forms in waterlogged conditions.

Perlite - A lightweight, porous volcanic rock that is often used as a horticultural growing medium.

Pesticide - A substance used for destroying insects or other organisms harmful to cultivated plants or to animals.
pH level - The measurement of acidity or alkalinity in the soil surrounding a plant's roots.

Photoperiod cannabis - Varieties of the cannabis plant that rely on changes in the duration of light and darkness to initiate and regulate flowering.

Plant saucer - A shallow, circular dish placed under a potted plant to catch water draining from the bottom of the container, preventing water from seeping onto surfaces and protecting floors from potential water damage.

Plat tray - A larger, shallow container designed to hold multiple pots, efficiently collecting excess water from various plants.

Potting soil / potting mix - A mixture of peat moss and other organic materials such as perlite, vermiculite, compost, and worm castings.

PPF (Photosynthetic Photon Flux) - Measures the total amount of photosynthetically active photons emitted by a light source, typically expressed in micromoles per second (μmol/s).

PPFD (Photosynthetic Photon Flux Density) - Measures the intensity of photosynthetically active photons hitting a specific surface area, typically expressed in micromoles per square meter per second ($\mu mol/m^2/s$).

Raised bed - An elevated gardening area often constructed from wood or stone.

Rhizodeposits - Organic compounds, such as sugars and amino acids, released by plant roots into the surrounding soil.

Rice hulls - The protective outer layer of rice grains, and they are often used in gardening as a lightweight and porous material.

Root bound - When a plant's roots outgrow their container, hindering growth and nutrient absorption.

Sowing - The act of planting seeds in soil or another growing medium to initiate the germination process and grow plants.

Secondary metabolites - Organic compounds produced by plants that are not directly involved in their primary metabolic processes, such as growth and development.

Soil - A mixture of organic matter, minerals, gases, liquids, and organisms that together support life of plants and soil organisms.

Soil food web - A complex network of interacting organisms in the soil, including bacteria, fungi, protozoa, nematodes, and other microorganisms, along with larger organisms like insects and earthworms.

Synthetic - Something produced through chemical or artificial processes rather than being naturally occurring.

Terpenes - A diverse class of organic compounds produced by various plants contributing to their distinct aromas and flavors.

Topsoil - A combination of sand or clay (ground-up rocks) mixed with organic materials such as compost.

Vapor Pressure Deficit (VPD) - The difference between the amount of moisture in the air and the maximum amount the air could hold at a specific temperature.

Vegetative stage - A plant's growth stage that is characterized by active foliage development, stem elongation, and the absence of flower or fruit production.

Windburn - A condition caused by exposure to strong winds, leading to desiccation and damage to the plant's foliage.

Worm castings - A nutrient-rich organic fertilizer and one of the most commonly used organic inputs in gardening.

Made in the USA
Las Vegas, NV
10 February 2024